Virginia SOL Grade 4 Mathematics Secrets

Study Guide
Your Key to Exam Success

Virginia SOL Test Review for the
Virginia Standards of Learning Examination

Dear Future Exam Success Story:

Congratulations on your purchase of our study guide. Our goal in writing our study guide was to cover the content on the test, as well as provide insight into typical test taking mistakes and how to overcome them.

Standardized tests are a key component of being successful, which only increases the importance of doing well in the high-pressure high-stakes environment of test day. How well you do on this test will have a significant impact on your future- and we have the research and practical advice to help you execute on test day.

The product you're reading now is designed to exploit weaknesses in the test itself, and help you avoid the most common errors test takers frequently make.

How to use this study guide

We don't want to waste your time. Our study guide is fast-paced and fluff-free. We suggest going through it a number of times, as repetition is an important part of learning new information and concepts.

First, read through the study guide completely to get a feel for the content and organization. Read the general success strategies first, and then proceed to the content sections. Each tip has been carefully selected for its effectiveness.

Second, read through the study guide again, and take notes in the margins and highlight those sections where you may have a particular weakness.

Finally, bring the manual with you on test day and study it before the exam begins.

Your success is our success

We would be delighted to hear about your success. Send us an email and tell us your story. Thanks for your business and we wish you continued success-

Sincerely,

Mometrix Test Preparation Team

TABLE OF CONTENTS

Numbers, Operations, and Quantitative Reasoning

Least to greatest and writing out numbers

<u>Example 1</u>
Write each list of numbers from least to greatest, and write each number in words:
  a) 4,002; 280; 108,511; 9
  b) 5,075,000,600; 190,800,330; 7,000,300,001

a) 4,002: four thousand two; 280: two hundred eighty; 08,511: one hundred eight thousand five hundred eleven; 9: nine;

b) 5,075,000,600: five billion seventy five million six hundred; 190,800,330: one hundred ninety million eight hundred thousand three hundred thirty; 7,000,300,001: seven million three hundred thousand and one

<u>Example 2</u>
Write each list of numbers from least to greatest, and write each decimal in words:
  a) 0.06; 6.0; 0.6
  b) 0.11; 0.09; 0.43

a) 0.06: six hundredths; 0.6: six tenths; 6.0: six
b) 0.09: nine hundredths; 0.11: eleven hundredths; 0.43: forty-three hundredths

Place value

Write the place value of each digit in the following number: 14,059.82

1: ten thousands
4: thousands
0: hundreds
5: tens
9: ones
8: tenths
2: hundredths

Fraction strip

<u>Example 1</u>
Use a fraction strip to find a fraction equal to: $\frac{5}{8}$.

First, draw a fraction strip equal to the given fraction. Draw 8 equally-sized spaces, and shade 5 of them to represent $\frac{5}{8}$.

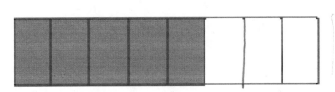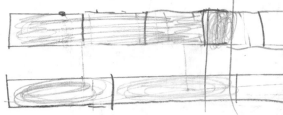

Next, divide each of the eight spaces into smaller spaces. For example, each of the eight spaces can be divided into two smaller spaces. The divisions are represented as dashed lines.

Find the total number of new spaces, and the number of the new spaces that are shaded. Write this as a fraction to represent a fraction equal to $\frac{5}{8}$.

$$\frac{\#\ shaded\ spaces}{\#\ total\ spaces} = \frac{10}{16}$$

Example 2

A cookie recipe asks for $1\frac{1}{2}$ sticks of butter. Draw the butter needed for the recipe.

Each stick of butter can be represented with a rectangle. Draw a rectangle to represent the first stick of butter. Since more than one whole stick is needed in the recipe, shade this entire stick to show that it is used in the recipe.

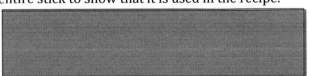

Draw a second rectangle to represent the additional butter needed in the recipe. The whole stick is not needed. Only the remaining butter, the $\frac{1}{2}$ stick, will be used. Divide the stick into two equal pieces, and shade one of the pieces to show the $\frac{1}{2}$ stick used in the recipe.

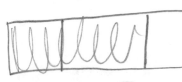

Example 3

Use fraction strips to determine which fraction is greater: $\frac{2}{3}$ or $\frac{3}{5}$.

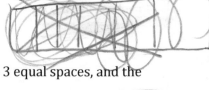

Draw two fraction strips that are the same size. Divide the first into 3 equal spaces, and the second into 5 equal spaces.

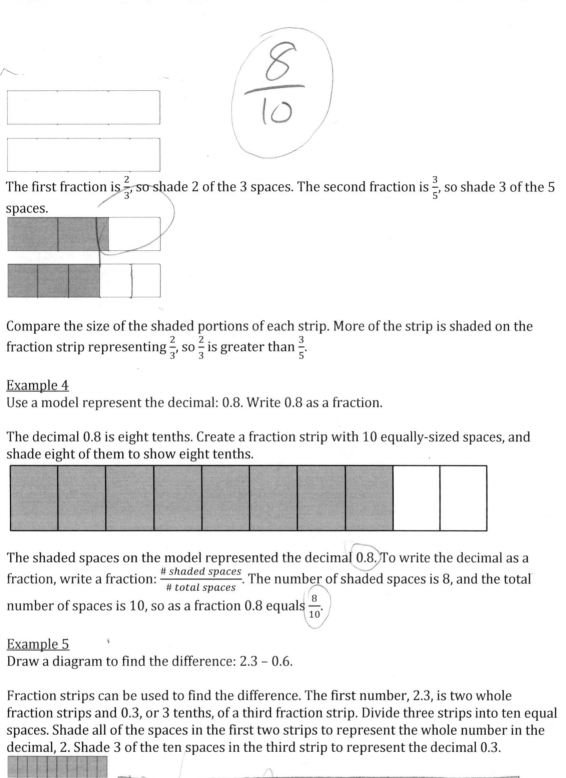

$\frac{8}{10}$

The first fraction is $\frac{2}{3}$, so shade 2 of the 3 spaces. The second fraction is $\frac{3}{5}$, so shade 3 of the 5 spaces.

Compare the size of the shaded portions of each strip. More of the strip is shaded on the fraction strip representing $\frac{2}{3}$, so $\frac{2}{3}$ is greater than $\frac{3}{5}$.

Example 4
Use a model represent the decimal: 0.8. Write 0.8 as a fraction.

The decimal 0.8 is eight tenths. Create a fraction strip with 10 equally-sized spaces, and shade eight of them to show eight tenths.

The shaded spaces on the model represented the decimal 0.8. To write the decimal as a fraction, write a fraction: $\frac{\#\ shaded\ spaces}{\#\ total\ spaces}$. The number of shaded spaces is 8, and the total number of spaces is 10, so as a fraction 0.8 equals $\frac{8}{10}$.

Example 5
Draw a diagram to find the difference: 2.3 – 0.6.

Fraction strips can be used to find the difference. The first number, 2.3, is two whole fraction strips and 0.3, or 3 tenths, of a third fraction strip. Divide three strips into ten equal spaces. Shade all of the spaces in the first two strips to represent the whole number in the decimal, 2. Shade 3 of the ten spaces in the third strip to represent the decimal 0.3.

To subtract 0.6, or 6 tenths, take 6 of the tenths away from the fraction strips. Three of the tenths can be taken from the fraction strip with only 3 shaded tenths. Take another 3 away from one of the strips with all ten spaces shaded.

- 3 -

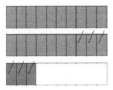

One whole fraction strip, and 7 tenths of a second are left, which is the mixed number: 1.7, so: 2.3 − 0.6 = 1.7.

Fraction circles

Alex's mom brings $6\frac{3}{4}$ oranges to a soccer game. Draw the number of oranges she brought to the game.

The whole number is the number of whole oranges brought to the game. Each of these can be represented by a circle. Shade the entire circle to show the whole orange was used.

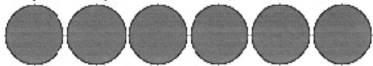

The fraction of an orange is only a portion of a circle. Divide a circle into three equal spaces, and shade two of them to represent the $\frac{3}{4}$ of an orange.

Writing numbers as fractions

<u>Example</u>
A six-sided die is rolled 60 times. The results are recorded in the table below.

Side	Number of times rolled
1	8
2	11
3	9
4	6
5	12
6	14

Write each result as a fraction of the total results.

To write the results of each side as a fraction of the total results, write the number of times the side was rolled in the numerator and the total number of rolls in the denominator.

Side	Number of times rolled
1	$\dfrac{8}{60}$
2	$\dfrac{11}{60}$
3	$\dfrac{9}{60}$
4	$\dfrac{6}{60}$
5	$\dfrac{12}{60}$
6	$\dfrac{14}{60}$

Model to represent decimals

Use a model to represent the decimal: 0.24. Write 0.24 as a fraction.

The decimal 0.24 is twenty four hundredths. One possible model to represent this fraction is to draw 100 pennies, since each penny is worth 1 one hundredth of a dollar. Draw one hundred circles to represent one hundred pennies. Shade 24 of the pennies to represent the decimal twenty four hundredths.

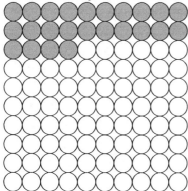

To write the decimal as a fraction, write a fraction: $\dfrac{\#\ shaded\ spaces}{\#\ total\ spaces}$. The number of shaded spaces is 24, and the total number of spaces is 100, so as a fraction 0.24 equals $\dfrac{24}{100}$.

Subtracting money

Chris brings $20.00 to the store. He spends $2.00 on a notebook. Determine how much money Chris has remaining after his purchase.

To find how much money Chris has left after his purchase, subtract the amount of the purchase from the total amount of money Chris had before he made his purchase.
Money before purchase – cost of purchase = money remaining
$20.00 – $2.00 = $18.00.

Multiplication

Ms. Webber collects pictures from her students to create a yearbook. The yearbook is 15 pages long, and there are 4 pictures on each page. Find the total number of pictures in the yearbook.

To find the total number of pictures, multiply the number of pictures on each page by the number of pages. If there are 4 pictures on each page, and a total of 15 pages, then the total number of pictures in the yearbook is: $4 \cdot 15 = 60$. Addition can also be used to find the total number of pictures. If there are 15 pages, then add 4 fifteen times to find the total number of pictures on the 15 pages:
4 + 4 + 4 + 4 + 4 + 4 + 4 + 4 + 4 + 4 + 4 + 4 + 4 + 4 + 4 = 60 pictures.

Addition

Lindsay and April both bring balloons to a birthday party. Lindsay brings 14 balloons, and April brings 8 balloons. Find the total number of balloons the girls brought to the party.

To find the total number of balloons, add together the balloons brought by each girl.
Lindsay's balloons + April's balloons = 14 + 8 = 22 balloons
The girls brought a total of 22 balloons to the party.

Addition of money

Christian has $0.40, and Allison has $0.80. Determine how much money they have altogether.

To find out how much money Christian and Allison have altogether, add together the money that each person has. To help add the money, the decimals can be represented using coins. Since each dime is $0.10, $0.40 is equal to 4 dimes, and $0.80 is equal to 8 dimes. Draw circles to represent the dimes.
Christian:

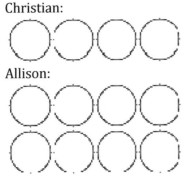

Allison:

To find the total money they have altogether, count the total dimes. There are 12 dimes. If each dime is worth $0.10, the total money that Christian and Allison have is $1.20.

Area model for multiplication

Use an area model to find the product: 8 · 10.

To find the product using an area model, draw a rectangle that is 8 units high and 10 units wide.

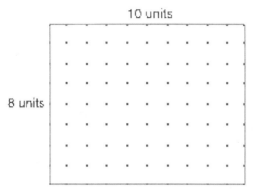

To find the product: 8 · 10, count the squares inside the area of the rectangle. There are 80 squares, so: 8 · 10 = 80.

Array for multiplication

Use an array to find the product: 7 · 7.

To find the product using an array, draw 7 rows and 7 columns of circles.

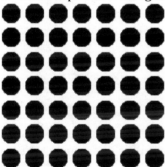

The total number of circles is the product: 7 · 7. There are 49 circles, so: 7 · 7 = 49.

Diagram for division

Mrs. Jan purchased pencils for her students. There are 10 students, and she purchased 40 pencils. If she wants to give each student the same number of pencils, find the number of pencils she should give to each student.

A diagram can be used to solve the problem. Mrs. Jan is dividing the total number of pencils, 40, by the total number of students, 10, to find the number of pencils for each student: 40 ÷ 10. Draw 40 pencils using line segments, then divide the pencils into groups of 10.

If 40 pencils are divided into groups of 10, there will be four total groups. Mrs. Jan should give each student 40 ÷ 10 = 4 pencils.

Finding products

<u>Example 1</u>
Write a problem that could be solved by finding the product: 4 · 6:

An example situation is: there are four students, and each student has six notebooks. Find the total number of notebooks. To find the total number of notebooks, multiply the number of students, 4, by the number of notebooks that each student has, 6: 4 · 6 = 24.

<u>Example 2</u>
Find the following products:
1) 2 · 6
2) 5 · 3
3) 7 · 9
4) 4 · 11
5) 12 · 10

Recall multiplication facts to find each product.
1) 2 · 6 = 12
2) 5 · 3 = 15
3) 7 · 9 = 63
4) 4 · 11 = 44
5) 12 · 10 = 120

<u>Example 3</u>
Ms. Webber collects pictures from her students to create a yearbook. The yearbook is 15 pages long, and there are 4 pictures on each page. Find the total number of pictures in the yearbook.

To find the total number of pictures, multiply the number of pictures on each page by the number of pages. If there are 4 pictures on each page, and a total of 15 pages, then the total number of pictures in the yearbook is: 4 · 15 = 60.

<u>Example 4</u>
A teacher estimates that it will take him 12 minutes to grade each student's test. He gave a test to 56 students. Determine how long it will take the teacher to grade all of the tests.

To find the total time, in minutes, that it will take the teacher to grade all of the tests, multiply the time it takes to grade each test by the number of students whose tests need to be graded. It takes 12 minutes to grade each test, and there are 56 students who took a test. The total time to grade all tests is: 12 minutes per test · 56 student tests = 672 minutes.

Division problems

Example 1
T-shirts are sold in packages of multiple shirts. Four t-shirts are sold in one package for $8.00. Five t-shirts are sold in a second package for $15.00. Compare the price of a single t-shirt from the two packages.

To find the price of each t-shirt, divide the quantity of shirts in each package by the cost of each package. The cost of each shirt should be rounded to the nearest cent, or hundredth, since this is the smallest unit of dollars.

Package 1: $\frac{\$8.00}{4} = \$2.00$

Package 2: $\frac{\$15.00}{5} = \$3.00$

The price per t-shirt is cheaper if purchasing the four t-shirts for $8.00.

Example 2
The fifth graders decide to hold a car wash to earn $810.00 for a class field trip. The students will earn $6.00 for each car that is washed. Find the number of cars that need to be washed to earn $810.00.

To find the number of cars the students need to wash, divide the total amount needed by the amount earned for each car that is washed. The students need to earn $810.00, and earn $6.00 for each car, so the total number of cars that need be washed is: $\frac{\$810.00}{\$6.00} = 135$. The total number of cars that need to be washed is 135.

Problems containing both multiplication and division

Example 1
Mason is ordering chocolate candies to give to 12 friends. He wants to give each friend 6 pieces of chocolate. The candies come in bags of 10. Determine how many bags of candy Mason needs to order.

First, find the total candies that Mason needs. The total candies is the number of friends, 12, times the number of candies for each friend 6: $12 \cdot 6 = 72$. Next, find the number of bags he should order. Since the candies come in bags of 10, round the total number of candies needed up to the nearest 10; 72 rounded up to the nearest 10 is 80. The number of bags to order is the total candies ordered, 80, divided by the number of candies in each bag, 10: $80 \div 10 = 8$. Mason needs to order 8 bags of candy.

Example 2
A store sells printer paper in packages of 100 sheets. Mrs. Fay is printing a test for her students. Each test needs 10 sheets of paper, and she has 54 total students. Determine how many packages of paper she should buy.

First, find the total sheets of paper she needs. The total sheets of paper needed is the sheets needed per student, 10, times the number of students, 54: $10 \cdot 54 = 540$. Next, find the number of sheets of paper she should buy. Since the paper comes in packages of 100, round the total sheets needed up to the nearest 100; 540 rounded to the nearest 100 is 600. The number of packages to buy is the total pages, 600, divided by the number of sheets in each package, 100: 600 ÷ 100 = 6. Mrs. Fay needs to order 6 packages of paper.

Patterns, Relationships, and Algebraic Reasoning

Fact family

Write the fact family for each equation.
- 1) $4 \cdot 3 = 12$
- 2) $8 \cdot 9 = 72$
- 3) $12 \div 6 = 2$

A fact family is the set of equations that use the same three numbers in the original equation. The equations will contain either multiplication or division.

1) $4 \cdot 3 = 12$
$3 \cdot 4 = 12$
$12 \div 3 = 4$
$12 \div 4 = 3$

2) $8 \cdot 9 = 72$
$9 \cdot 8 = 72$
$72 \div 9 = 8$
$72 \div 8 = 9$

3) $12 \div 6 = 2$
$12 \div 2 = 6$
$2 \cdot 6 = 12$
$6 \cdot 2 = 12$

Columns of information

Example 1

Describe how to find the number in column B using the number in column A. Find the number in column B for these values of A: 5, 6, 7, 8.

A	B
1	10
2	20
3	30
4	40

The number in column B is 10 times the number in column A:
$1 \cdot 10 = 10$
$2 \cdot 10 = 20$
$3 \cdot 10 = 30$
$4 \cdot 10 = 40$

The numbers in column be are going up by 10 as the numbers in column A go up by 1. 5 is one more than 4. To find the number in column B for when 5 is in column A, add 10 to the number in column B for A: 40 + 10 = 50. For any new

A	B
1	10
2	20
3	30
4	40
5	40 + 10 = 50
6	50 + 10 = 60
7	60 + 10 = 70
8	70 + 10 = 80

Example 2
The table below is the value of each part of an ordered pair. An ordered pair is written as: (x, y).

x	y
2	6
4	12
6	18
8	24

The value of y can be found if you know the value of x. The number in the y column is three times the number in the x column. Multiply the x number by 3 to get the y number.

x	y
2	$2 \cdot 3 = 6$
4	$4 \cdot 3 = 12$
6	$6 \cdot 3 = 18$
8	$8 \cdot 3 = 24$

Geometry and Spatial Reasoning

Right, acute, and obtuse angles

A right angle has a measure of 90º.

90º

An acute angle has a measure less than 90º.

An obtuse angle has a measure greater than 90º.

Parallel and perpendicular lines

Parallel lines are lines that never intersect.

Perpendicular lines are lines that intersect at a right angle.

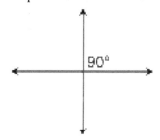

90º

Square

A square is a figure with equal side lengths and angle measures. The congruent components are the parts of the square that are the same size. A square has four sides that are the same length. The angles of a square also have same measure.

For example:

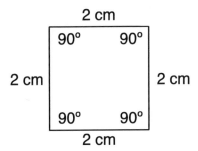

Parallelogram

A parallelogram is a quadrilateral where pairs of opposite sides are parallel. Opposite sides of a parallelogram are congruent, and opposite angles are also congruent. For example:

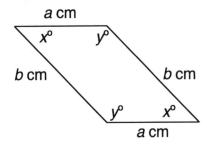

Rectangular prism

A rectangular prism is a three-dimensional figure with sides that are all rectangles.

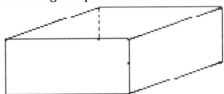

Translation

Create a congruent triangle to the one below by translating the triangle.

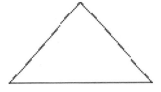

To create a congruent triangle by translating, move the figure left, right, up, or down. The congruent figure below, with the dashed lines, was moved up and to the right.

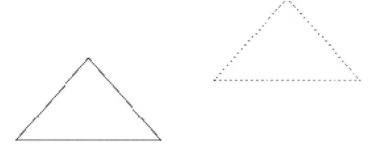

Reflection

Create a congruent rectangle to the one below by reflecting the rectangle.

To create a congruent rectangle by reflecting, first draw a line of reflection. The line can be next to or on the figure. Then draw the image reflected across this line.

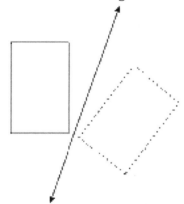

Rotation

Create a congruent triangle to the one below by rotating the triangle.

To create a congruent triangle by rotating, first draw a point of rotation. The point can be outside, inside, or on the figure. Then pick a number of degrees to rotate the figure. For example, rotate the figure 90º.

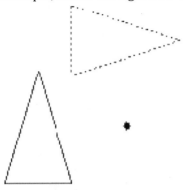

Symmetry

If a figure has symmetry, a line of symmetry can be drawn in the figure. On either side of the line of symmetry, the pieces of the figure are congruent.
For example:

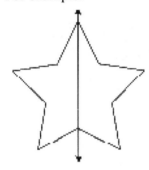

Reflection to find line of symmetry

If a figure is reflected across a line of symmetry, the new figure should be congruent to the original figure and in the same position. For example, a figure identical to the original can be created by reflecting across the line of symmetry below.

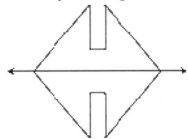

Measurement

Perimeter and area of a rectangle

A rectangle has a length of 3 units and a width of 1 unit. Find the perimeter and area of the rectangle.

Draw a model of the rectangle with the given dimensions.

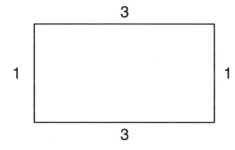

The perimeter of a rectangle is the sum of side lengths: perimeter = 3 units + 1 unit + 3 units + 1 unit = 8 units.

The area of a rectangle measures the space inside the rectangle. To find the measure of this space, find the product of the rectangle's length and width: area = 3 units · 1 units = 3 units².

Conversion of measurements

Example 1
There are 100 cm in 1 m. Convert between the measurements below.
a) 1.4 m in cm
b) 218 cm in m

Write a ratio relating the units: $\frac{100\ cm}{1\ m}$. Use the ratio to write a proportion to convert the given units.

a)
$$\frac{100\ cm}{1\ m} = \frac{x\ cm}{1.4\ m}$$

$x = 140$
1.4 m = 140 cm

b)
$$\frac{100\ cm}{1\ m} = \frac{218\ cm}{x\ m}$$

$100x = 218$
$x = 2.18$
218 cm = 2.18 m

<u>Example 2</u>
There are 12 inches in 1 foot, and 3 feet in 1 yard. Convert between the measurements below.
a) 42 inches to feet
b) 15 feet to yards

Write a ratio relating the units: $\frac{12\ in}{1\ ft}$ and $\frac{3\ ft}{1\ yd}$. Use the ratios to write a proportion to convert the given units.

a)
$$\frac{12\ in}{1\ ft} = \frac{42\ in}{x\ ft}$$
$12x = 42$
$x = 3.5$
42 inches = 3.5 feet

b)
$$\frac{3\ ft}{1\ yd} = \frac{15\ ft}{x\ yd}$$
$3x = 15$
$x = 5$
15 feet = 5 yards

Volume

<u>Example 1</u>
The figure below is divided into cubes. Each cube has a volume of 1 unit³. Find the volume of the rectangular prism.

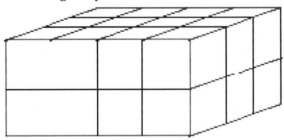

To find the volume of the rectangular prism, find the number of cubes in the figure. The figure has two layers of cubes. On the top layer, the number of cubes can be counted. There are 12 cubes on the top layer. The bottom layer is the same as the top, so there are also 12 cubes in the bottom layer. There are 24 total cubes in the figure, so the volume of the figure is 24 units³.

<u>Example 2</u>
Explain how to find the volume of a rectangular prism with a length of 2 units, a width of 6 units, and a height of 3 units.

Draw a model of the rectangular prism with the given dimensions.

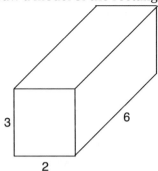

The volume of a rectangular prism measures the space inside the prism. To find the size of the space, first find the area of any face of the prism. For example, find the area of the bottom of the prism. The length of the bottom is 2 units and the width is 6 units, so the area is: $2 \cdot 6 = 12$ units^2. Then, multiply this area by the third dimension, to get a measure of the interior of the prism: 12 units$^2 \cdot 3$ units $= 36$ units^3.

Mass and weight

The mass of an object is a measure of how much matter the object contains. The mass of an object is always the same. The weight of an object is a measure of how heavy it is. The weight changes depending on the gravity of the place where the weight is measured. For example, an object on the earth and an object on the moon have the same mass. On earth, the object would weigh more than the object on the moon because the gravity on the earth is stronger than the gravity on the moon.

Temperature

Find the temperature, in degrees Fahrenheit, on the thermometer below. Use the thermometer to find the temperature if the temperature increased by 5º Fahrenheit.

The temperature, on the thermometer, is 75º F. If the temperature increases by 5º F, change the thermometer to show the increase in 5º:

If the temperature increases by 5º F, the new temperature is 80º F.

Time

Lindsay leaves for school at 7:00am. It takes her 20 minutes to get to school. Use a clock to determine the time Lindsay arrives at school.

7:00 am means the large clock hand is on 12, and the small hand is on 7.

In 20 minutes, the big hand will move 20 minutes clockwise, to the 4. The big hand will also move closer to the 8. 20 minutes is: $\frac{20}{60} = \frac{1}{3}$ of an hour, so the big hand will move one third of the way from the 7 to the 8.

The ending time is 7:20am, which is when Lindsay arrives at school.

Probability and Statistics

Number of combinations

Ted picks his clothing in the morning from a selection of 4 pairs of pants and 3 shirts. Draw a diagram to find the number of possible combinations of a single pair of pants and a single shirt.

A tree diagram can be used to find the number of different ways pants and shirts can be combined.

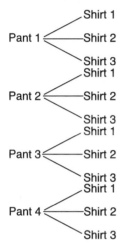

There are twelve different combinations of pants and shirts.

Bar graph

A class records data when students are born. Draw a bar graph to represent the data in the table below.

Month born	Number of students
January	3
February	5
March	2
April	1
May	0
June	4
July	1
August	0
September	4
October	6
November	5
December	3

To draw a bar graph, first create horizontal and vertical axes. The horizontal axis will be the month, and the vertical axis will be the number of students. Draw rectangles at each month, showing the number of students born in each month.

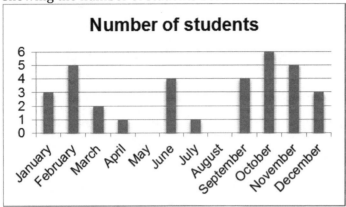

Interpreting a bar graph

List the types of pet in order of most popular to least popular.

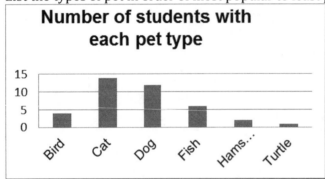

The pet with the highest number of students is the most popular. 14 students have cats, 12 students have dogs, 6 students have fish, 4 have birds, 2 have hamsters, and 1 has a turtle. From most to least popular the pets are: cats, dogs, fish, birds, hamsters, turtles.

Practice Test #1

Practice Questions

1. Which of the following is written in order from *greatest to least*, when reading from left to right?

a. 44,982,016	5,221,415	782,498	586,301	69,309
b. 782,498	5,221,415	586,301	44,982,016	69,309
c. 782,498	69,309	5,221,415	586,301	44,982,016
d. 5,221,415	44,982,016	782,498	586,301	69,309

2. Donald has the amount of money shown below. How much money does he have?

    a. $6.14
    b. $6.19
    c. $6.24
    d. $6.29

3. Which of the following models represents a fraction equivalent to $\frac{2}{5}$?

    a.
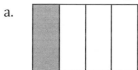

    b.
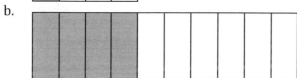

    c.
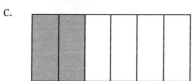

    d.
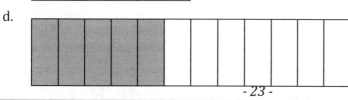

- 23 -

4. Which fraction is represented by the diagram shown below?

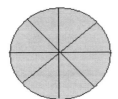 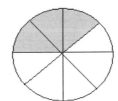

   a. $1\frac{1}{8}$

   b. $1\frac{1}{4}$

   c. $1\frac{3}{8}$

   d. $1\frac{1}{2}$

5. Which of the following models represents a fraction less than the fraction shown below?

a.

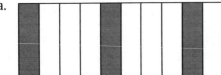

b.

c.

d.

6. Suppose each flat represents one unit. What number if represented below?

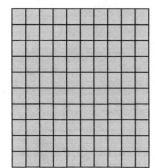 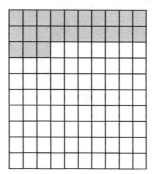

    a. 12.3
    b. 1.23
    c. 0.123
    d. 100.23

7. Jasper collects 1,082 cans of food. He gives a certain number of cans to the first local charity he finds. He now has 602 cans of food. How many cans of food did he give to the first local charity?
    a. 430
    b. 480
    c. 682
    d. 1,684

8. Amanda creates the base of a picture frame, using 4.55 inches of red fabric and 6.25 inches of blue fabric. How many inches of fabric are used to create the base of the frame?
    a. 10.80 inches
    b. 10.85 inches
    c. 10.75 inches
    d. 10.90 inches

9. In multiplying 14 by 5, using the area model shown below, how many tens "rods" will be included in the product section of the model?

    a. 4
    b. 5
    c. 9
    d. 10

10. Which of the following number sentences is represented by the array shown below?

X X X X X
X X X X X
X X X X X
X X X X X

a. $4 + 6 = 10$
b. $4 \times 6 = 24$
c. $24 - 6 = 18$
d. $24 \div 3 = 8$

11. Which of the following number sentences is represented by the model shown below?

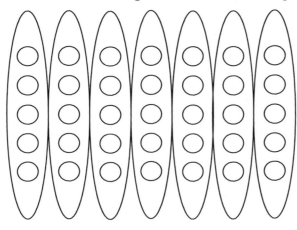

a. $7 \times 7 = 49$
b. $35 - 7 = 28$
c. $7 + 5 = 12$
d. $35 \div 7 = 5$

12. Hannah ran 12 laps every day for 8 days. How many laps did she run in all?
a. 108
b. 96
c. 84
d. 72

13. Kevin approved 13 trees out of every group of trees he surveyed. He surveyed 15 groups of trees. How many trees did he approve?
a. 155
b. 165
c. 195
d. 205

14. Monique has $690 to spend on a 3-day trip. She plans to spend an equal amount of money per day. How many dollars can she spend per day?

```
┌─────┬─────┬─────┐
│     │     │     │
├─────┼─────┼─────┤
│ (0) │ (0) │ (0) │
│ (1) │ (1) │ (1) │
│ (2) │ (2) │ (2) │
│ (3) │ (3) │ (3) │
│ (4) │ (4) │ (4) │
│ (5) │ (5) │ (5) │
│ (6) │ (6) │ (6) │
│ (7) │ (7) │ (7) │
│ (8) │ (8) │ (8) │
│ (9) │ (9) │ (9) │
└─────┴─────┴─────┘
```

15. Three friends sold cupcakes for a fundraiser. Eli sold 84 cupcakes, John sold 46 cupcakes, and Kim sold 72 cupcakes. Which of the following is the best estimate for the number of cupcakes the three friends sold in all?
  a. 180
  b. 200
  c. 210
  d. 190

16. Lynn has $316 to spend on groceries for the month. He plans to spend the same amount of money on groceries each week. Which of the following is the best estimate for the amount of money he can spend on groceries each week?
  a. $65
  b. $75
  c. $90
  d. $95

17. Carlisle charges $21.95 per hair cut and has completed 30 haircuts this week. Which of the following is the best approximation for the total charges for all haircuts?
  a. $450
  b. $600
  c. $750
  d. $800

18. Which of the following number sentences belongs in the fact family shown below?
$$7 \times 6 = 42$$
$$6 \times 7 = 42$$
$$42 \div 7 = 6$$
  a. $7 + 6 = 13$
  b. $42 \div 6 = 7$
  c. $42 + 7 = 49$
  d. $42 - 6 = 36$

19. What is the 11th number in the pattern shown below?
    10, 20, 30, 40, ...
    a. 90
    b. 100
    c. 110
    d. 120

20. What is the 8th number in the pattern shown below?
    108, 96, 84, 72, ...
    a. 48
    b. 36
    c. 24
    d. 12

21. Mrs. Thompson writes the number sentences shown below:
    $100 \times 13 = 1300$
    $100 \times 14 = 1400$
    $100 \times 15 = 1500$
    $100 \times 24 = ?$

What is the product of the last number sentence?
    a. 2200
    b. 2300
    c. 2400
    d. 2500

22. The number of sit-ups Aisha has completed over a period of 3 days is shown in the table below.

Day	Number of Sit-ups
1	35
2	70
3	105

If this pattern continues, how many sit-ups will she have completed after 7 days?

23. Which of the following correctly describes the relationship between the values of x and y, as shown in the table below?

x	y
1	4
2	8
3	12
4	16

    a. The value of x is 6 less than the value of y
    b. The value of y is 4 times the value of x
    c. The value of y is 4 more than the value of x
    d. The value of x is 1 less than the value of y

24. Which of the following correctly describes an acute angle?
    a. An angle with a measure greater than 90 degrees
    b. An angle with a measure greater than 180 degrees
    c. An angle with a measure less than 120 degrees
    d. An angle with a measure less than 90 degrees

25. Which of the following statements is true?
    a. The measure of an acute angle is greater than the measure of a right angle, but less than the measure of an obtuse angle
    b. The measure of a right angle is greater than the measure of an acute angle, but less than the measure of an obtuse angle
    c. The measure of an obtuse angle is less than the measure of a right angle, but greater than the measure of an acute angle
    d. The measure of an obtuse angle is less than the measure of an acute angle, but greater than the measure of a right angle

26. Which of the following pairs of lines are parallel?

a.

b.

c.

d.

27. Which of the following best describes the pair of lines shown below?

a. perpendicular
b. parallel
c. intersecting and perpendicular
d. intersecting

28. Which of the following figures has a square base and four triangular faces?
    a. cube
    b. triangular prism
    c. square pyramid
    d. triangular pyramid

29. Which of the following figures has 8 edges?
    a. triangular prism
    b. cube
    c. square pyramid
    d. triangular pyramid

30. Which shape has 5 sides?
    a. hexagon
    b. pentagon
    c. octagon
    d. heptagon

31. Which shape is defined using the statement shown below?
A shape with four congruent sides and four right angles
    a. square
    b. rhombus
    c. parallelogram
    d. rectangle

32. A triangle is rotated about one of its vertices. Which of the following statements is true?
    a. The rotated triangle is similar to, but not congruent to, the original triangle
    b. The rotated triangle is congruent to the original triangle
    c. The rotated triangle is not similar to or congruent to the original triangle
    d. The rotated triangle is larger than the original triangle

33. The shape below represents a reflection about the axis. Which of the following statements is true?

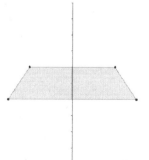

    a. The shape has one line of symmetry
    b. The shape has two lines of symmetry
    c. The shape has four lines of symmetry
    d. The shape does not have any lines of symmetry

34. What number is represented by Point A, shown on the number line below?

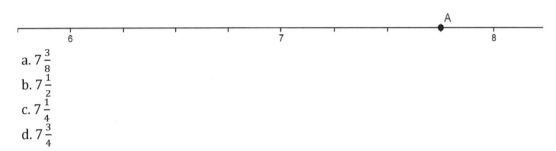

a. $7\frac{3}{8}$

b. $7\frac{1}{2}$

c. $7\frac{1}{4}$

d. $7\frac{3}{4}$

35. Which point, on the number line below, represents $14\frac{2}{10}$?

a. Point A
b. Point B
c. Point C
d. Point D

36. A clock is shown below. Use the ruler from your mathematics chart to measure the width of the face of the clock, from one edge to the other. Which of the following best represents the width of the face?

a. 4 centimeters
b. 7 centimeters
c. 9 centimeters
d. 11 centimeters

37. Which of the following is the most reasonable estimate for the length of a book?

    a. $\frac{1}{2}$ meter

    b. $11\frac{1}{2}$ inches

    c. 8 millimeters

    d. 2 yards

38. Which of the following is the most reasonable estimate for the weight of a chair?

    a. 1 ton

    b. 15 pounds

    c. 3 kilograms

    d. 6 grams

39. Ana paints a line that is 14 feet, in length. How long is the painted line, in inches?

40. Kevin's baby drinks 64 ounces of milk each day. How many pints of milk does his baby drink each day?

    a. 2

    b. 4

    c. 8

    d. 12

41. A box has a length of 7.5 inches, a width of 3.85 inches, and a height of 2.3 inches. Which of the following best represents the volume of the box?

    a. 28 in³
    a. 28 in^3

    b. 36 in^3

    c. 48 in^3

    d. 64 in^3

42. Which of the following units is used to measure mass?

    a. gram

    b. inch

    c. pound

    d. centiliter

43. Aubrey arrived at the party at the time shown on the clock below. It is now four-thirty. How much time has passed since she arrived at the party?

    a. 1 hour, 45 minutes
    b. 2 hours, 5 minutes
    c. 2 hours, 15 minutes
    d. 2 hours, 30 minutes

44. Kelsey surveys her classmates to determine their favorite types of music. The results are shown in the table below.

Type of Music	Number of Students
Classical	7
Rock	8
Blues	11
Country	4
Other	10

Which circle graph correctly represents the results?

a.

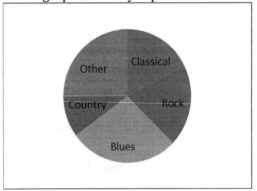

c.

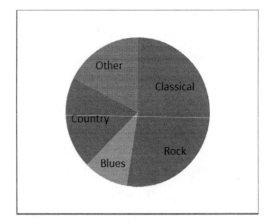

b.

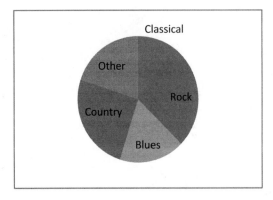

d.

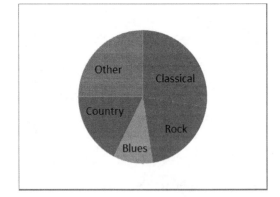

45. The yearly earnings (in dollars) for a local business are represented by the line graph below.

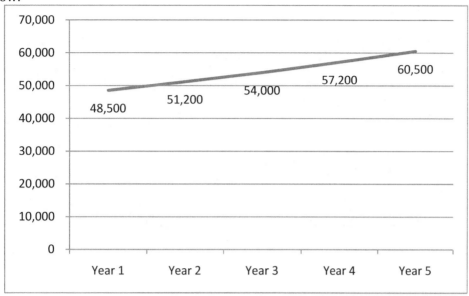

Which of the following is the best estimate for the company's revenue in Year 8?
    a. $64,000
    b. $69,000
    c. $75,000
    d. $78,000

46. The bar graph below represents student preferences for different parks in Flagstaff, Arizona.

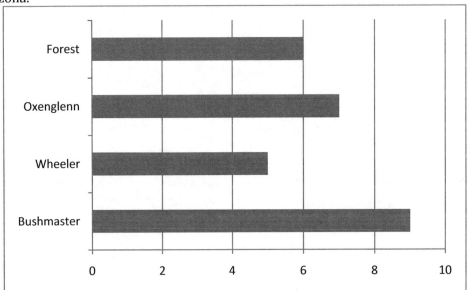

Which park is preferred by the most students?
   a. Bushmaster
   b. Wheeler
   c. Oxenglenn
   d. Forest

47. A cafeteria offers 3 meats, 3 vegetables, 2 breads, and 2 desserts. How many possible meal combinations are there?

48. The average number of miles per hour driven by a sample of drivers is shown below.
65, 70, 60, 55, 70, 65, 70, 60, 65, 70, 55, 65, 70, 55, 60

Based on the data, which average speed is driven by the most drivers?

a. 55
b. 60
c. 65
d. 70

Answers and Explanations

1. A: The number, 44,982,016, is the greatest because it has a value in the ten millions place. This number is followed by 5,221,415, which has a value in the millions place. The number, 782,498, is greater than 586,301 because the 7 in the hundred thousands of the first number is greater than the 5 in the hundred thousand place in the second number. The number, 69,309, is least because it only goes up to the ten thousands place value.

2. C: Donald has five dollar bills, which totals $5, and $1.24 in change; the sum of $5 and $1.24 is $6.24.

3. B: The fraction, $\frac{2}{5}$, is equivalent to the fraction, $\frac{4}{10}$. The numerator and denominator of the given fraction are both multiplied by 2 to obtain the model for $\frac{4}{10}$; the fractions are proportional.

4. C: The diagram represents one whole, plus three-eighths of a second whole. Therefore, the diagram represents the fraction, $1\frac{3}{8}$.

5. B: The given model represents the fraction, $\frac{2}{9}$, which is approximately 0.22. The model for Choice B represents the fraction, $\frac{1}{8}$, which equals 0.125. This fraction is less than the given fraction. The fractions can also be compared by finding a least common denominator.

6. B: Since each flat represents one unit, the first flat represents 1, whereas the second flat represents $\frac{23}{100}$, or 0.23. Together, the diagram represents the number, 1.23.

7. B: In order to find the number of cans of food he gave to the first charity, the number of cans of food he has left needs to be subtracted from the number of cans he collected; $1,082 - 602 = 480$.

8. A: The sum of the two decimals is 10.80; the decimals are added just like whole numbers are, while aligning the decimal point.

9. B: Five tens "rods" will fit in the product section of the model. The rods will be placed to the right of the rod, shown in the diagram, underneath the five ones "units" at the top of the model.

10. B: The array represents the multiplication sentence, $4 \times 6 = 24$. Note. There are 4 rows and 6 x's in each row.

11. D: The model shows 35 counters, divided into 7 groups, with 5 counters in each group. Therefore, the model represents the number sentence, $35 \div 7 = 5$.

12. B: She runs 12×8 laps in all, or 96 laps.

13. C: Since he approved 13 trees out of every group of trees and surveyed 15 groups, he approved 13×15 trees, or 195 trees.

14. The correct answer is 230: In order to find the amount of money she can spend each day, 690 should be divided by 3; $690 \div 3 = 230$. Thus, she can spend 230 dollars per day.

15. B: The number of cupcakes sold can be rounded as follows: 80 cupcakes, 50 cupcakes, and 70 cupcakes, which sum to 200. Therefore, the best estimate for the number of cupcakes sold is 200 cupcakes.

16. B: The amount of money Lynn has to spend on groceries for the month can be rounded to $300; $300 \div 4 = 75$. Thus, the best estimate for the amount of money he can spend per week is $75.

17. B: The amount of money Carlisle charges per hair cut can be rounded to $20; $20 \times 30 = 600$. Thus, his total charges are approximately $600.

18. B: The missing number sentence in the fact family is the other division number sentence, which reads: $42 \div 6 = 7$.

19. C: The value of each number in the pattern is a multiple of 10. Therefore, the 11th number represents the value of the product of 11 and 10; $11 \times 10 = 110$.

20. C: The pattern represents a sequence that subtracts 12 from each previous term. The first number in the pattern represents the product of 9 and 12; $9 \times 12 = 108$. The eighth number in the pattern is 7 numbers away from the first number of 108. Thus, the eighth number represents the product of 2 and 12, which equals 24. The eighth number in the pattern is 24. The eighth number in the pattern can also be found by subtracting 12 from the last given number in the pattern 4 more times; $72 - 12 = 60$; $60 - 12 = 48$; $48 - 12 = 36$; $36 - 12 = 24$.

21. C: As noted in the pattern, the product of 100 and 24 can be found by multiplying 24 by 1 and adding two zeros to the product. Thus, the product of 100 and 24 is 2400.

22. 245. Since she completes 35 each day, she has completed 35×7 situps after 7 days; $35 \times 7 = 245$.

23. B: The value of y is indeed 4 times the value of x. Note. 4 is 4 times the value of 1; 8 is 4 times the value of 2; 12 is 4 times the value of 3; and 16 is 4 times the value of 4.

24. D: An acute angle has a measure less than 90 degrees.

25. B: A right angle has a measure of 90 degrees, which is greater than the measure of an acute angle, with an angle less than 90 degrees. A right angle also has a measure less than the measure of an obtuse angle, which has a measure greater than 90 degrees.

26. A: Parallel lines are lines that do not intersect and are the same distance apart.

27. D: The lines shown are intersecting, but they are not perpendicular; they do not form a right angle.

28. C: A square pyramid has a square base and four triangular faces.

- 39 -

29. C: A square pyramid has four edges on the base and one edge, coming from each vertex of the base.

30. B: A pentagon has 5 sides.

31. A: A square has four congruent sides and four right angles. A rhombus has four congruent sides, but is not required to have four right angles.

32. B: A rotation does not change the shape and size of a shape. Therefore, the rotated triangle is congruent to the original triangle.

33. A: The trapezoid is symmetric about the axis, thus showing at least one line of symmetry. The isosceles trapezoid does not have any more lines of symmetry. Therefore, it has one line of symmetry.

34. D: The number line is divided into fourths. Thus, between the whole numbers, 7 and 8, lie the fractions, $7\frac{1}{4}, 7\frac{2}{4}$, and $7\frac{3}{4}$. Point A represents the fraction, $7\frac{3}{4}$.

35. B: The number line is divided into tenths. Thus, between the whole numbers, 14 and 15, lie the fractions, $14\frac{1}{10}, 14\frac{2}{10} \ldots 14\frac{9}{10}$. The fraction, $14\frac{2}{10}$, lies two-tenths, or two intervals, to the right of 14.

36. B: The width of the face is approximately 7 cm, as measured from one edge of the face of the clock to the other edge.

37. B: The length of a book is possibly $11\frac{1}{2}$ inches; one-half of a meter is 50 centimeters, which would be almost 2 feet; 8 millimeters is less than 1 centimeter; and 2 yards is equal to 6 feet. None of the other measurements are likely for a book length.

38. B: A chair may possibly weigh 15 pounds; 1 ton is equal to 2,000 pounds; 3 kilograms is equal to 3,000 grams; and 6 grams is the weight of about 12 pencils.

39. 168: The length of the painted line, in inches, is equal to the product of 14 and 12; $14 \times 12 = 168$. Thus, the painted line is 168 inches, in length.

40. B: There are 8 ounces in each cup of milk, so 64 ounces is equal to 8 cups. Since there are 2 cups in a pint, there are 8 cups in 4 pints. Thus, his baby drinks 4 pints of milk each day.

41. D: The measurements of the box can be rounded to 8 inches, 4 inches, and 2 inches. The volume of the box is equal to the product of the measurements of the length, width, and height of the box. Thus, the volume is approximately $8 \times 4 \times 2$, or 64 cubic inches.

42. A: Mass can be measured in grams, whereas weight can be measured in pounds. Inches measure length, and centiliters measure capacity.

43. C: From 2:15 to 4:15, two hours have passed. From 4:15 to 4:30, 15 additional minutes have passed. Therefore, the elapsed time is 2 hours, 15 minutes.

44. A: The circle graph can be created by determining the fraction of students, with preferences for each type of music. The total number of students surveyed is 40. Thus, 7 out of 40 students, or $\frac{7}{40}$ students, prefer classical music; 8 out of 40 students, or $\frac{8}{40}$ students, prefer rock music; 11 out of 40 students, or $\frac{11}{40}$ students, prefer blues; 4 out of 40 students, or $\frac{4}{40}$ students, prefer country; and 10 out of 40 students, or $\frac{10}{40}$ students, prefer other music. These fractions can be converted to the following percentages: approximately 18% prefer classical music, 20% prefer rock music, approximately 28% prefer blues, 10% prefer country, and 25% prefer other music. The circle graph, shown for Choice A, correctly represents these percentages.

45. B: The revenue, from year to year, increases by approximately $3,000. Thus, a good estimate for Year 6 would be $63,500, while a good estimate for Years 7 and 8 would be $66,500 and $69,500. The estimate for Choice B, of $69,000, is a good estimate for Year 8. Note. Some yearly changes were less than $3,000, while other yearly changes were more than $3,000.

46. A: There were 9 students who preferred Bushmaster Park; 9 students is more than any other number of students displayed on the bar graph.

47. 36. The possible meal combinations are equal to the product of the number of different types of each part of the meal. Thus, the possible meal combinations are equal to $3 \times 3 \times 2 \times 2$, or 36.

48. D: Five drivers drove at an average speed of 70 miles per hour, which is more than any other number of drivers, driving at a particular speed; three drivers drove at an average speed of 55 miles per hour, three drivers drove at an average speed of 60 miles per hour, and four drivers drove at an average speed of 65 miles per hour.

Practice Test #2

Practice Questions

1. The number of miles driven per year, by five sales professionals, is listed below.

19,802   24,321   26,094   24,283   18,002

Which of the following lists the number of miles driven per year, in order from least to greatest, when reading from left to right?
   a. 18,002   19,802   24,283   24,321   26,094
   b. 24,283   24,321   18,002   19,802   26,094
   c. 26,094   24,283   24,321   18,002   19,802
   d. 19,802   24,283   24,321   18,002   26,094

2. Which of the following numbers is less than 802,430,298?
   a. 802,428,986
   b. 802,460,999
   c. 802,431,304
   d. 802,539,002

3. Amanda buys a sandwich and pays the amount of money shown below. How much does she pay?

   a. $3.56
   b. $3.61
   c. $3.50
   d. $3.51

4. Which of the following sets represents a fraction equivalent to $\frac{8}{12}$?

a.

b.

c.

d.

5. Which of the following models represents a fraction equal to the fraction shown below?

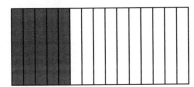

a.

b.

c.

d.

- 43 -

6. Which fraction is represented by the diagram shown below?

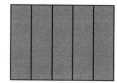 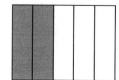

    a. $1\frac{1}{2}$

    b. $1\frac{2}{5}$

    c. $1\frac{3}{5}$

    d. $1\frac{3}{4}$

7. How much of the flat shown below is shaded?

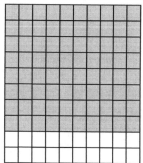

    a. $\frac{3}{5}$

    b. $\frac{3}{4}$

    c. $\frac{4}{5}$

    d. $\frac{2}{3}$

8. Martin saved $156 in September, $173 in October, and $219 in November. How much money did he save during the three months?

    a. $538

    b. $569

    c. $548

    d. $576

9. Andrea pays $120 more in rent per month this year than she did last year. She pays $763 per month this year. How much did she pay per month last year?

    a. $663

    b. $643

    c. $863

    d. $883

10. Which sum is represented by the diagram shown below?

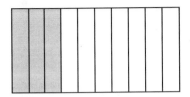 +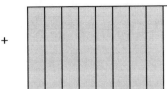

    a. 1.08
    b. 1.09
    c. 1.10
    d. 1.11

11. Kelsey multiplies 18 by 6, using the area model shown below. How many unit "squares" will she include in the product section of the model?

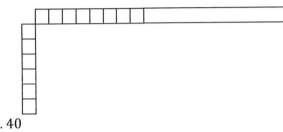

    a. 40
    b. 46
    c. 48
    d. 54

12. Which fact is represented by the array shown below?

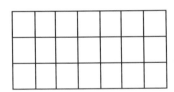

    a. $3 + 7 = 10$
    b. $21 - 7 = 14$
    c. $3 \times 7 = 21$
    d. $10 + 7 = 17$

13. Eli has 42 crayons and plans to give the same number of crayons to each of his 6 friends. Which number sentence can be used to find the number of crayons he will give to each friend?
    a. $42 - 6 = 36$
    b. $42 \div 6 = 7$
    c. $42 \times 6 = 252$
    d. $42 + 6 = 48$

14. Alex buys 3 gallons of milk each week. How many gallons of milk does he buy in 12 weeks?
    a. 18
    b. 24
    c. 36
    d. 48

15. A candle-making shop sold 18 candles on Friday, 37 candles on Saturday, and 23 candles on Sunday. Which of the following is the best estimate for the number of candles sold during the three days?
    a. 60
    b. 70
    c. 80
    d. 90

16. Isabelle must drive 1,482 miles. She plans to drive approximately the same number of miles per day over the period of 5 days. Which of the following is the best approximation for the number of miles she will drive per day?
    a. 250
    b. 300
    c. 350
    d. 400

17. A consultant earned $17,850 over the course of 6 months. Which of the following is the best approximation for the amount of money the consultant earned each month?
    a. $2,500
    b. $3,000
    c. $3,500
    d. $4,000

18. Mr. Jacobsen writes the number sentences shown below:
    $8 \times 9 = 72$
    $9 \times 8 = 72$
    $72 \div 9 = 8$
What is the fourth number sentence of this fact family?
    a. $8 + 9 = 17$
    b. $72 - 8 = 64$
    c. $72 \div 8 = 9$
    d. $17 - 9 = 8$

19. What is the 14th number in the pattern shown below?
        100, 200, 300, 400, ...
    a. 1,200
    b. 1,300
    c. 1,400
    d. 1,500

20. What is the 12th number in the pattern shown below?
    11, 22, 33, 44, ...

0	0	0
1	1	1
2	2	2
3	3	3
4	4	4
5	5	5
6	6	6
7	7	7
8	8	8
9	9	9

21. The number of miles Brad has driven over a period of 3 days is shown in the table below.

Day	Number of Miles
1	275
2	550
3	825

If this pattern continues, how many miles will he have driven after 8 days?
    a. 2,000
    b. 2,025
    c. 2,075
    d. 2,200

22. Andrew displays the following sets of data to his colleagues. Which of the following represents the relationship between the first and second columns of data?

4	16
7	19
12	24
14	26
19	31

    a. The values in the second column are 12 more than the values in the first column.
    b. The values in the first column are one-fourth of the values in the second column.
    c. The values in the first column are 11 fewer than the values in the second column.
    d. The values in the second column are 3 more than the values in the first column.

23. A local citizen represents the total amount she has donated to a charity over the course of five years, using the table shown below.

Year	1	2	3	4	5
Amount Donated	$250	$550	$850	$1,150	$1,450

If this pattern continues, how much will she have donated after 10 years?
    a. $2,850
    b. $2,900
    c. $2,950
    d. $3,000

24. Morris needs to define an obtuse angle. Which of the following correctly describes the requirements for such an angle?
    a. An angle with a measure greater than 180 degrees
    b. An angle with a measure greater than 120 degrees
    c. An angle with a measure less than 90 degrees
    d. An angle with a measure greater than 90 degrees

25. Which of the following angles is acute?
    a.

    b.

    c.

    d.

26.Which of the following most accurately describes the pair of lines shown below?

a. Lines that do not intersect
b. Lines that intersect
c. Lines that do not intersect and remain the same distance apart
d. Lines that are perpendicular

27. Which of the following represents perpendicular lines?

a.

b.

c.

d.

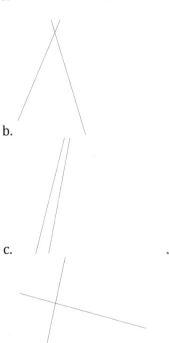

28. Which of the following figures has 5 vertices?
   a. triangular prism
   b. square pyramid
   c. rectangular prism
   d. triangular pyramid

29. Which of the following figures has 4 faces?
   a. cube
   b. triangular pyramid
   c. triangular prism
   d. square pyramid

30. Which of the following figures has more than 6 vertices?
   a. triangular prism
   b. cube
   c. triangular pyramid
   d. square pyramid

31. Which shape has 4 perpendicular and congruent sides?
   a. rhombus
   b. parallelogram
   c. square
   d. rectangle

32. Triangle ABC is translated as shown below.

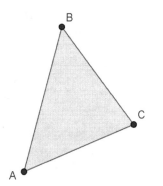 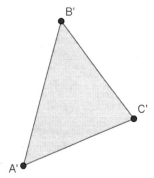

Which of the following correctly describes the two triangles?
   a. The translated triangle is not similar to or congruent to the original triangle.
   b. The translated triangle has been stretched.
   c. The translated triangle is congruent to the original triangle.
   d. The translated triangle is similar to, but not congruent to, the original triangle.

33. The triangle graphed below represents a reflection about the axis. How many lines of symmetry does the triangle have?

a. 0
b. 1
c. 2
d. 3

34. What decimal is represented by Point P, shown on the number line below?

a. 5.6
b. 5.7
c. 5.8
d. 5.9

35. What fraction is represented by Point A, shown on the number line below?

a. $3\frac{1}{4}$
b. $3\frac{2}{3}$
c. $3\frac{1}{2}$
d. $3\frac{3}{4}$

36. A die is shown below. Which of the following best represents the volume of the die?

a. 12 cm³
b. 27 cm³
c. 64 cm³
d. 125 cm³

37. A scaled drawing of a barn is shown below. Use the ruler from your mathematics chart to measure the length of the barn. Which of the following best represents the length of the barn, in the drawing?

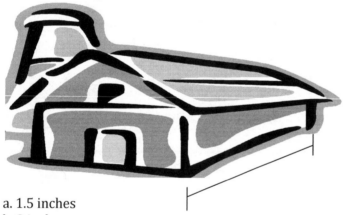

a. 1.5 inches
b. 2 inches
c. 2.5 inches
d. 3 inches

38. Which of the following is the most reasonable estimate for the capacity of a bathtub?
a. 5 liters
b. 100 milliliters
c. 25 gallons
d. 180 ounces

39. Which of the following is the most reasonable estimate for the weight of a pencil?
a. 12 ounces
b. 0.5 ounces
c. 2 pounds
d. 0.5 pounds

40. Hannah weighs approximately 27 pounds. What is her approximate weight, in ounces?
   a. 432 ounces
   b. 378 ounces
   c. 324 ounces
   d. 438 ounces

41. Jamal drinks 2 quarts of water per day. How many cups of water does he drink?

42. A gift box has a length of 18 inches, a width of 12 inches, and a height of 8 inches. Which of the following is the best estimate for the volume of the box?
   a. 2,400 in^3
   b. 2,000 in^3
   c. 1,200 in^3
   d. 2,800 in^3

43. Elaine left for work at the time shown on the clock below. It is now 9:25. How much time has passed, since she left for work?

7:3

   a. 1 hour, 35 minutes
   b. 1 hour, 40 minutes
   c. 1 hour, 45 minutes
   d. 1 hour, 50 minutes

44. Anand surveys his classmates to determine their favorite season of the year. The results are shown in the table below.

Season	Number of Students
Fall	7
Winter	3
Spring	12
Summer	18

Which circle graph correctly represents the results?

a.
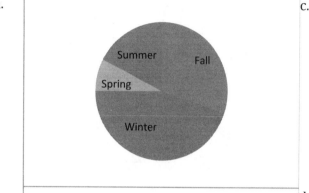

c.
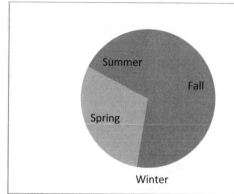

b.
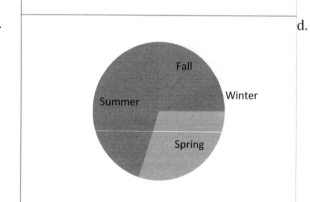

d.
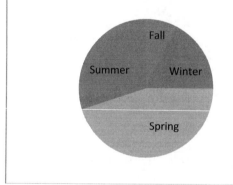

45. The number of cars sold per year, by a local dealership, is represented by the line graph below.

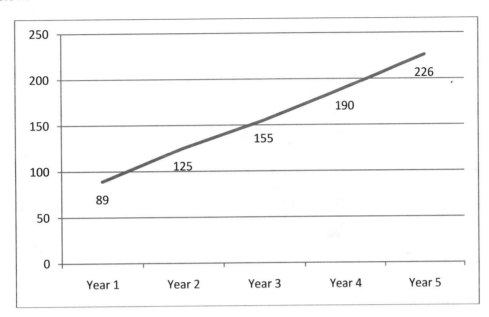

Which of the following is the best estimate for the number of cars the dealership will sell in Year 9?
    a. 306
    b. 366
    c. 426
    d. 506

46. The bar graph below represents teacher preferences for different vacation states.

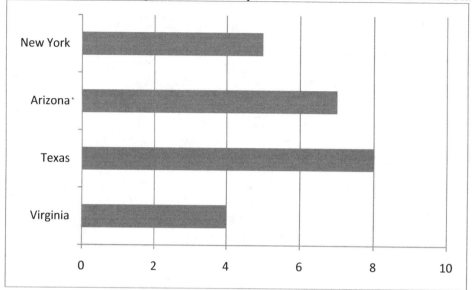

Which state was preferred by the fewest number of teachers?
    a. Virginia
    b. Arizona
    c. Texas
    d. New York

47. Alana can choose from 2 shirts, 2 pairs of jeans, 3 pairs of socks, and 2 pairs of shoes. How many possible outfit combinations can she make?

0	0
1	1
2	2
3	3
4	4
5	5
6	6
7	7
8	8
9	9

48. The scores on Mrs. Rodriguez's math test are shown below.
    95, 78, 92, 99, 74, 83, 89, 92, 79, 85, 87, 90, 88, 92, 79
    Which test score was received by the most students?
    a. 78
    b. 90
    c. 92
    d. 79

Answers and Explanations

1. A: The numbers can first be compared by examining the value of the number in the ten thousands place; 18,002 and 19,802 are less than 24,283, 24,321, and 26,094; 18,002 is less than 19,802 because the 8 in the thousands place, in 18,002, is less than the 9 in the thousands place, in 19,802; 24,283 is less than 24,321 because the 2 in the hundreds place, in 24,283, is less than the 3 in the hundreds place, in 24,321; 26,094 has the greatest value.

2. A: The number, 802,428,986, is less than 802,430,298 because the 2 in the ten thousands place, in 802,428,986, is less than the 3 in the ten thousands place, in 802,430,298.

3. D: The amount of money she pays is equal to the sum of 3 dollar bills, or $3, and 51 cents, or $0.51. Thus, she paid $3.51 for the sandwich.

4. B: The fraction, $\frac{8}{12}$, is equivalent to the fraction, $\frac{2}{3}$. The numerator and denominator of the given fraction are both divided by 4 to obtain the model for $\frac{2}{3}$; the fractions are proportional.

5. B: The fraction, $\frac{5}{15}$, is equivalent to the fraction, $\frac{1}{3}$. The numerator and denominator of the given fraction are both divided by 5 to obtain the model for $\frac{1}{3}$; the fractions are proportional.

6. B: The first diagram represents 1 whole, while the second diagram represents $\frac{2}{5}$. Thus the diagram represents $1\frac{2}{5}$, in its entirety.

7. C: The flat is $\frac{8}{10}$ shaded, which is 0.80; $\frac{4}{5} = 0.80$. Also, $\frac{8}{10}$ reduces to $\frac{4}{5}$.

8. C: The sum of the dollar amounts is equal to $156 + $173 + $219, or $548.

9. B: Since Andrea paid $120 per month more last year, the amount she paid per month last year is equal to the difference of $763 and $120, or $643.

10. C: The diagram represents the sum of $\frac{3}{10}$ and $\frac{8}{10}$, or $\frac{11}{10}$, which is equivalent to $1\frac{1}{10}$, or 1.10. The decimals, 0.30 + 0.80, can also be added, which equal 1.10.

11. C: Forty-eight unit "squares" will fit in the product section of the model. The squares will be placed to the right of the ones "units", shown on the left side of the diagram and underneath the six ones "units" at the top of the model; $6 \times 8 = 48$.

12. C: The array includes 3 rows and 7 columns. Thus, the array represents the number sentence, $3 \times 7 = 21$.

13. B: Since Eli will equally share his crayons, he will divide 42 crayons into 6 groups; $42 \div 6 = 7$.

14. C: Alex will be 3×12 gallons of milk in 12 weeks, or 36 gallons of milk.

15. C: The number of candles sold can be rounded as follows: 20 candles, 40 candles, and 20 candles. Thus, a good estimate of the number of candles sold is 20 + 40 + 20 candles, or 80 candles.

16. B: The distance Isabelle drives can be rounded to 1,500 miles; 1,500 miles divided by 5 days is equal to 300 miles driven per day.

17. B: The consultant's earnings can be rounded to $18,000; $18,000 divided over 6 months is equal to $3,000 per month.

18. C: The missing number sentence in the fact family is the other division number sentence, which reads: $72 \div 8 = 9$.

19. C: The value of each number in the pattern is a multiple of 100. Therefore, the 14th number represents the value of the product of 14 and 100; $14 \times 100 = 1400$.

20. 132. The value of each number in the pattern is a multiple of 11. Therefore, the 12th number represents the value of the product of 12 and 11; $12 \times 11 = 132$.

21. D: Brad drives 275 miles each day. Thus, the total number of miles driven, over a period of days, can be found by adding 275 miles to the number of total miles driven for each previous day. In other words, after 4 days, he drove 1,100 miles. After 5 days, he drove 1,375 miles. After 6 days, he drove 1,650 miles. After 7 days, he drove 1,925 miles. After 8 days, he drove 2,200 miles.

22. A: The values in the second column are indeed 12 more than the values in the first column. Note. 16 is 12 more than 4; 19 is 12 more than 7; 24 is 12 more than 12; 26 is 12 more than 14; and 31 is 12 more than 19.

23. C: The total amount of money donated is $300 more each additional year. Thus, the total amount donated, over a period of years, can be found by adding 300 dollars to the amount donated for each previous year. In other words, after 6 years, the total amount donated was $1,750. After 7 years, the total amount donated was $2,050. After 8 years, the total amount donated was $2,350. After 9 years, the total amount donated was $2,650. After 10 years, the total amount donated was $2,950.

24. D: An obtuse angle has a measure greater than 90 degrees. It may be greater than 120 degrees, but that is not a requirement.

25. A: An acute angle has a measure less than 90 degrees. The angle shown for Choice A is indeed less than 90 degrees (or the measure of a right angle).

26. C: The lines are parallel and do not intersect. However, the most accurate description includes the fact that the lines remain the same distance apart. Note. Lines may not intersect and not be parallel.

27. D: Perpendicular lines form four right angles, or 90 degree angles. The lines shown for Choice D form four right angles.

28. B: A square pyramid has 5 vertices, with 4 at the base of the pyramid and 1 at the top.

29. B: A triangular pyramid has 4 faces, with 1 triangular face at the base and 3 more triangular faces.

30. B: A cube has 8 vertices, with 4 vertices at the top of the cube and 4 more vertices at the bottom of the cube.

31. C: A square has 4 congruent sides that are perpendicular to one another, forming 4 right angles. A rhombus is not required to have perpendicular sides.

32. C: A translated figure is always congruent to the original figure because the size, shape, and angle measures do not change. A translation is simply a slide up, down, right, or left, or a combination of these slides.

33. B: The triangle is symmetric about the axis, thus showing at least one line of symmetry. The isosceles triangle does not have any more lines of symmetry. Therefore, it has one line of symmetry.

34. C: The number line is divided into tenths. Thus, between the whole numbers, 5 and 6, lie the decimals, 5.1, 5.2, 5.3, 5.4, 5.5, 5.6, 5.7, 5.8, and 5.9. Point P represents the decimal, 5.8.

35. D: The number line is divided into fourths. Thus, between the whole numbers, 3 and 4, lie the fractions, $3\frac{1}{4}, 3\frac{2}{4}$, and $3\frac{3}{4}$. Point A represents the fraction, $3\frac{3}{4}$.

36. B: Each side of the cube is approximately 3 cm. Thus, the approximate volume of the cube is equal to $3 \times 3 \times 3$, or 27 cubic centimeters.

37. A: The barn measures approximately 1.5 inches, in length.

38. C: A normal bathtub holds approximately 25 gallons of water, give or take some gallons. The other choices are much too small.

39. B: A pencil weighs approximately one-half of an ounce. The other choices are too heavy, in measurement.

40. A: There are 16 ounces in one pound. Thus, her approximate weight, in ounces, is equal to the product of 27 and 16; $27 \times 16 = 432$. She weighs approximately 432 ounces.

41. 08. There are 2 cups in 1 pint and 2 pints in 1 quart. There are 4 pints in 2 quarts. Thus, there are 4×2, or 8 cups, in 2 quarts.

42. B: The dimensions of the box round to 20 inches, 10 inches, and 10 inches. The volume of a box can be determined by finding the product of the dimensions. Thus, the approximate volume is equal to $20 \times 10 \times 10$, or 2,000 cubic inches.

43. D: From 7:35 to 8:35, one hour has passed. From 8:35 to 9:25, 50 additional minutes have passed. Therefore, the elapsed time is 1 hour, 50 minutes.

44. B: The circle graph can be created by determining the fraction of students, with preferences for each season. The total number of students surveyed is 40. Thus, 7 out of 40

students, or $\frac{7}{40}$ students, prefer Fall; 3 out of 40 students, or $\frac{3}{40}$ students, prefer Winter; 12 out of 40 students, or $\frac{12}{40}$ students, prefer Spring; and 18 out of 40 students, or $\frac{18}{40}$ students, prefer Summer. These fractions can be converted to the following percentages: approximately 18% prefer Fall, approximately 8% prefer Winter, 30% prefer Spring, and 45% prefer Summer. The circle graph, shown for Choice B, correctly represents these percentages.

45. B: The dealership sells approximately 35 more cars each year. So, a good estimate would be 261 cars sold in Year 6, 296 cars sold in Year 7, 331 cars sold in Year 8, and 366 cars sold in Year 9.

46. A: There were 4 teachers who preferred Virginia; 4 teachers is less than any other number of teachers displayed on the bar graph.

47. 24. The possible outfit combinations are equal to the product of the number of different types of each clothing piece. Thus, the possible outfit combinations are equal to $2 \times 2 \times 3 \times 2$, or 24.

48. C: The score of 92 was received by 3 students, which is more than any other score received; 78 was received by 1 student; 90 was received by 1 student; and 79 was received by 2 students.

Secret Key #1 - Time is Your Greatest Enemy

Pace Yourself

Wear a watch. At the beginning of the test, check the time (or start a chronometer on your watch to count the minutes), and check the time after every few questions to make sure you are "on schedule."

If you are forced to speed up, do it efficiently. Usually one or more answer choices can be eliminated without too much difficulty. Above all, don't panic. Don't speed up and just begin guessing at random choices. By pacing yourself, and continually monitoring your progress against your watch, you will always know exactly how far ahead or behind you are with your available time. If you find that you are one minute behind on the test, don't skip one question without spending any time on it, just to catch back up. Take 15 fewer seconds on the next four questions, and after four questions you'll have caught back up. Once you catch back up, you can continue working each problem at your normal pace.

Furthermore, don't dwell on the problems that you were rushed on. If a problem was taking up too much time and you made a hurried guess, it must be difficult. The difficult questions are the ones you are most likely to miss anyway, so it isn't a big loss. It is better to end with more time than you need than to run out of time.

Lastly, sometimes it is beneficial to slow down if you are constantly getting ahead of time. You are always more likely to catch a careless mistake by working more slowly than quickly, and among very high-scoring test takers (those who are likely to have lots of time left over), careless errors affect the score more than mastery of material.

Secret Key #2 - Guessing is not Guesswork

You probably know that guessing is a good idea - unlike other standardized tests, there is no penalty for getting a wrong answer. Even if you have no idea about a question, you still have a 20-25% chance of getting it right.

Most test takers do not understand the impact that proper guessing can have on their score. Unless you score extremely high, guessing will significantly contribute to your final score.

Monkeys Take the Test

What most test takers don't realize is that to insure that 20-25% chance, you have to guess randomly. If you put 20 monkeys in a room to take this test, assuming they answered once per question and behaved themselves, on average they would get 20-25% of the questions correct. Put 20 test takers in the room, and the average will be much lower among guessed questions. Why?

1. The test writers intentionally write deceptive answer choices that "look" right. A test taker has no idea about a question, so picks the "best looking" answer, which is often wrong. The monkey has no idea what looks good and what doesn't, so will consistently be lucky about 20-25% of the time.
2. Test takers will eliminate answer choices from the guessing pool based on a hunch or intuition. Simple but correct answers often get excluded, leaving a 0% chance of being correct. The monkey has no clue, and often gets lucky with the best choice.

This is why the process of elimination endorsed by most test courses is flawed and detrimental to your performance- test takers don't guess, they make an ignorant stab in the dark that is usually worse than random.

$5 Challenge

Let me introduce one of the most valuable ideas of this course- the $5 challenge:

You only mark your "best guess" if you are willing to bet $5 on it.
You only eliminate choices from guessing if you are willing to bet $5 on it.

Why $5? Five dollars is an amount of money that is small yet not insignificant, and can really add up fast (20 questions could cost you $100). Likewise, each answer choice on one question of the test will have a small impact on your overall score, but it can really add up to a lot of points in the end.

The process of elimination IS valuable. The following shows your chance of guessing it right:

If you eliminate wrong answer choices until only this many remain:	Chance of getting it correct:
1	100%
2	50%
3	33%

However, if you accidentally eliminate the right answer or go on a hunch for an incorrect answer, your chances drop dramatically: to 0%. By guessing among all the answer choices, you are GUARANTEED to have a shot at the right answer.

That's why the $5 test is so valuable- if you give up the advantage and safety of a pure guess, it had better be worth the risk.

What we still haven't covered is how to be sure that whatever guess you make is truly random. Here's the easiest way:

Always pick the first answer choice among those remaining.

Such a technique means that you have decided, **before you see a single test question**, exactly how you are going to guess- and since the order of choices tells you nothing about which one is correct, this guessing technique is perfectly random.

This section is not meant to scare you away from making educated guesses or eliminating choices- you just need to define when a choice is worth eliminating. The $5 test, along with a pre-defined random guessing strategy, is the best way to make sure you reap all of the benefits of guessing.

Secret Key #3 - Practice Smarter, Not Harder

Many test takers delay the test preparation process because they dread the awful amounts of practice time they think necessary to succeed on the test. We have refined an effective method that will take you only a fraction of the time.

There are a number of "obstacles" in your way to succeed. Among these are answering questions, finishing in time, and mastering test-taking strategies. All must be executed on the day of the test at peak performance, or your score will suffer. The test is a mental marathon that has a large impact on your future.

Just like a marathon runner, it is important to work your way up to the full challenge. So first you just worry about questions, and then time, and finally strategy:

Success Strategy

1. Find a good source for practice tests.
2. If you are willing to make a larger time investment, consider using more than one study guide- often the different approaches of multiple authors will help you "get" difficult concepts.
3. Take a practice test with no time constraints, with all study helps "open book." Take your time with questions and focus on applying strategies.
4. Take a practice test with time constraints, with all guides "open book."
5. Take a final practice test with no open material and time limits

If you have time to take more practice tests, just repeat step 5. By gradually exposing yourself to the full rigors of the test environment, you will condition your mind to the stress of test day and maximize your success.

Secret Key #4 - Prepare, Don't Procrastinate

Let me state an obvious fact: if you take the test three times, you will get three different scores. This is due to the way you feel on test day, the level of preparedness you have, and, despite the test writers' claims to the contrary, some tests WILL be easier for you than others.
Since your future depends so much on your score, you should maximize your chances of success. In order to maximize the likelihood of success, you've got to prepare in advance. This means taking practice tests and spending time learning the information and test taking strategies you will need to succeed.

Never take the test as a "practice" test, expecting that you can just take it again if you need to. Feel free to take sample tests on your own, but when you go to take the official test, be prepared, be focused, and do your best the first time!

Secret Key #5 - Test Yourself

Everyone knows that time is money. There is no need to spend too much of your time or too little of your time preparing for the test. You should only spend as much of your precious time preparing as is necessary for you to get the score you need.

Once you have taken a practice test under real conditions of time constraints, then you will know if you are ready for the test or not.
If you have scored extremely high the first time that you take the practice test, then there is not much point in spending countless hours studying. You are already there.

Benchmark your abilities by retaking practice tests and seeing how much you have improved. Once you score high enough to guarantee success, then you are ready.

If you have scored well below where you need, then knuckle down and begin studying in earnest. Check your improvement regularly through the use of practice tests under real conditions. Above all, don't worry, panic, or give up. The key is perseverance!

Then, when you go to take the test, remain confident and remember how well you did on the practice tests. If you can score high enough on a practice test, then you can do the same on the real thing.

General Strategies

The most important thing you can do is to ignore your fears and jump into the test immediately- do not be overwhelmed by any strange-sounding terms. You have to jump into the test like jumping into a pool- all at once is the easiest way.

Make Predictions

As you read and understand the question, try to guess what the answer will be. Remember that several of the answer choices are wrong, and once you begin reading them, your mind will immediately become cluttered with answer choices designed to throw you off. Your mind is typically the most focused immediately after you have read the question and digested its contents. If you can, try to predict what the correct answer will be. You may be surprised at what you can predict.

Quickly scan the choices and see if your prediction is in the listed answer choices. If it is, then you can be quite confident that you have the right answer. It still won't hurt to check the other answer choices, but most of the time, you've got it!

Answer the Question

It may seem obvious to only pick answer choices that answer the question, but the test writers can create some excellent answer choices that are wrong. Don't pick an answer just because it sounds right, or you believe it to be true. It MUST answer the question. Once you've made your selection, always go back and check it against the question and make sure that you didn't misread the question, and the answer choice does answer the question posed.

Benchmark

After you read the first answer choice, decide if you think it sounds correct or not. If it doesn't, move on to the next answer choice. If it does, mentally mark that answer choice. This doesn't mean that you've definitely selected it as your answer choice, it just means that it's the best you've seen thus far. Go ahead and read the next choice. If the next choice is worse than the one you've already selected, keep going to the next answer choice. If the next choice is better than the choice you've already selected, mentally mark the new answer choice as your best guess.

The first answer choice that you select becomes your standard. Every other answer choice must be benchmarked against that standard. That choice is correct until proven otherwise by another answer choice beating it out. Once you've decided that no other answer choice seems as good, do one final check to ensure that your answer choice answers the question posed.

Valid Information

Don't discount any of the information provided in the question. Every piece of information may be necessary to determine the correct answer. None of the information in the question is there to throw you off (while the answer choices will certainly have information to throw you off). If two seemingly unrelated topics are discussed, don't ignore either. You can be confident there is a relationship, or it wouldn't be included in the question, and you are probably going to have to determine what is that relationship to find the answer.

Avoid "Fact Traps"

Don't get distracted by a choice that is factually true. Your search is for the answer that answers the question. Stay focused and don't fall for an answer that is true but incorrect. Always go back to the question and make sure you're choosing an answer that actually answers the question and is not just a true statement. An answer can be factually correct, but it MUST answer the question asked. Additionally, two answers can both be seemingly correct, so be sure to read all of the answer choices, and make sure that you get the one that BEST answers the question.

Milk the Question

Some of the questions may throw you completely off. They might deal with a subject you have not been exposed to, or one that you haven't reviewed in years. While your lack of knowledge about the subject will be a hindrance, the question itself can give you many clues that will help you find the correct answer. Read the question carefully and look for clues. Watch particularly for adjectives and nouns describing difficult terms or words that you don't recognize. Regardless of if you completely understand a word or not, replacing it with a synonym either provided or one you more familiar with may help you to understand what the questions are asking. Rather than wracking your mind about specific detailed information concerning a difficult term or word, try to use mental substitutes that are easier to understand.

The Trap of Familiarity

Don't just choose a word because you recognize it. On difficult questions, you may not recognize a number of words in the answer choices. The test writers don't put "make-believe" words on the test; so don't think that just because you only recognize all the words in one answer choice means that answer choice must be correct. If you only recognize words in one answer choice, then focus on that one. Is it correct? Try your best to determine if it is correct. If it is, that is great, but if it doesn't, eliminate it. Each word and answer choice you eliminate increases your chances of getting the question correct, even if you then have to guess among the unfamiliar choices.

Eliminate Answers

Eliminate choices as soon as you realize they are wrong. But be careful! Make sure you consider all of the possible answer choices. Just because one appears right, doesn't mean that the next one won't be even better! The test writers will usually put more than one good answer choice for every question, so read all of them. Don't worry if you are stuck between two that seem right. By getting down to just two remaining possible choices, your odds are now 50/50. Rather than wasting too much time, play the odds. You are guessing, but guessing wisely, because you've been able to knock out some of the answer choices that you know are wrong. If you are eliminating choices and realize that the last answer choice you are left with is also obviously wrong, don't panic. Start over and consider each choice again. There may easily be something that you missed the first time and will realize on the second pass.

Tough Questions

If you are stumped on a problem or it appears too hard or too difficult, don't waste time. Move on! Remember though, if you can quickly check for obviously incorrect answer choices, your chances of guessing correctly are greatly improved. Before you completely give up, at least try to knock out a couple of possible answers. Eliminate what you can and then guess at the remaining answer choices before moving on.

Brainstorm

If you get stuck on a difficult question, spend a few seconds quickly brainstorming. Run through the complete list of possible answer choices. Look at each choice and ask yourself, "Could this answer the question satisfactorily?" Go through each answer choice and consider it independently of the other. By systematically going through all possibilities, you may find something that you would otherwise overlook. Remember that when you get stuck, it's important to try to keep moving.

Read Carefully

Understand the problem. Read the question and answer choices carefully. Don't miss the question because you misread the terms. You have plenty of time to read each question thoroughly and make sure you understand what is being asked. Yet a happy medium must be attained, so don't waste too much time. You must read carefully, but efficiently.

Face Value

When in doubt, use common sense. Always accept the situation in the problem at face value. Don't read too much into it. These problems will not require you to make huge leaps of logic. The test writers aren't trying to throw you off with a cheap trick. If you have to go beyond creativity and make a leap of logic in order to have an answer choice answer the question, then you should look at the other answer choices. Don't overcomplicate the problem by creating theoretical relationships or explanations that will warp time or space. These are normal problems rooted in reality. It's just that the applicable relationship or explanation may not be readily apparent and you have to figure things out. Use your common sense to interpret anything that isn't clear.

Prefixes

If you're having trouble with a word in the question or answer choices, try dissecting it. Take advantage of every clue that the word might include. Prefixes and suffixes can be a huge help. Usually they allow you to determine a basic meaning. Pre- means before, post- means after, pro - is positive, de- is negative. From these prefixes and suffixes, you can get an idea of the general meaning of the word and try to put it into context. Beware though of any traps. Just because con is the opposite of pro, doesn't necessarily mean congress is the opposite of progress!

Hedge Phrases

Watch out for critical "hedge" phrases, such as likely, may, can, will often, sometimes, often, almost, mostly, usually, generally, rarely, sometimes. Question writers insert these hedge phrases to cover every possibility. Often an answer choice will be wrong simply because it leaves no room for exception. Avoid answer choices that have definitive words like "exactly," and "always".

Switchback Words

Stay alert for "switchbacks". These are the words and phrases frequently used to alert you to shifts in thought. The most common switchback word is "but". Others include although, however, nevertheless, on the other hand, even though, while, in spite of, despite, regardless of.

New Information

Correct answer choices will rarely have completely new information included. Answer choices typically are straightforward reflections of the material asked about and will directly relate to the question. If a new piece of information is included in an answer choice that doesn't even seem to relate to the topic being asked about, then that answer choice is likely incorrect. All of the information needed to answer the question is usually provided for you, and so you should not have to make guesses that are unsupported or choose answer choices that require unknown information that cannot be reasoned on its own.

Time Management

On technical questions, don't get lost on the technical terms. Don't spend too much time on any one question. If you don't know what a term means, then since you don't have a dictionary, odds are you aren't going to get much further. You should immediately recognize terms as whether or not you know them. If you don't, work with the other clues that you have, the other answer choices and terms provided, but don't waste too much time trying to figure out a difficult term.

Contextual Clues

Look for contextual clues. An answer can be right but not correct. The contextual clues will help you find the answer that is most right and is correct. Understand the context in which a phrase or statement is made. This will help you make important distinctions.

Don't Panic

Panicking will not answer any questions for you. Therefore, it isn't helpful. When you first see the question, if your mind goes blank, take a deep breath. Force yourself to mechanically go through the steps of solving the problem and using the strategies you've learned.

Pace Yourself

Don't get clock fever. It's easy to be overwhelmed when you're looking at a page full of questions, your mind is full of random thoughts and feeling confused, and the clock is ticking down faster than you would like. Calm down and maintain the pace that you have set for yourself. As long as you are on track by monitoring your pace, you are guaranteed to have enough time for yourself. When you get to the last few minutes of the test, it may seem like you won't have enough time left, but if you only have as many questions as you should have left at that point, then you're right on track!

Answer Selection

The best way to pick an answer choice is to eliminate all of those that are wrong, until only one is left and confirm that is the correct answer. Sometimes though, an answer choice may immediately look right. Be careful! Take a second to make sure that the other choices are not equally obvious. Don't make a hasty mistake. There are only two times that you should stop before checking other answers. First is when you are positive that the answer choice you have selected is correct. Second is when time is almost out and you have to make a quick guess!

Check Your Work

Since you will probably not know every term listed and the answer to every question, it is important that you get credit for the ones that you do know. Don't miss any questions through careless mistakes. If at all possible, try to take a second to look back over your answer selection and make sure you've selected the correct answer choice and haven't made a costly careless mistake (such as marking an answer choice that you didn't mean to mark). This quick double check should more than pay for itself in caught mistakes for the time it costs.

Beware of Directly Quoted Answers

Sometimes an answer choice will repeat word for word a portion of the question or reference section. However, beware of such exact duplication – it may be a trap! More than likely, the correct choice will paraphrase or summarize a point, rather than being exactly the same wording.

Slang

Scientific sounding answers are better than slang ones. An answer choice that begins "To compare the outcomes..." is much more likely to be correct than one that begins "Because some people insisted..."

Extreme Statements

Avoid wild answers that throw out highly controversial ideas that are proclaimed as established fact. An answer choice that states the "process should be used in certain situations, if..." is much more likely to be correct than one that states the "process should be discontinued completely." The first is a calm rational statement and doesn't even make a definitive, uncompromising stance, using a hedge word "if" to provide wiggle room, whereas the second choice is a radical idea and far more extreme.

Answer Choice Families

When you have two or more answer choices that are direct opposites or parallels, one of them is usually the correct answer. For instance, if one answer choice states "x increases" and another answer choice states "x decreases" or "y increases," then those two or three answer choices are very similar in construction and fall into the same family of answer choices. A family of answer choices is when two or three answer choices are very similar in construction, and yet often have a directly opposite meaning. Usually the correct answer choice will be in that family of answer choices. The "odd man out" or answer choice that doesn't seem to fit the parallel construction of the other answer choices is more likely to be incorrect.

Top 20 Test Taking Tips

1. Carefully follow all the test registration procedures
2. Know the test directions, duration, topics, question types, how many questions
3. Setup a flexible study schedule at least 3-4 weeks before test day
4. Study during the time of day you are most alert, relaxed, and stress free
5. Maximize your learning style; visual learner use visual study aids, auditory learner use auditory study aids
6. Focus on your weakest knowledge base
7. Find a study partner to review with and help clarify questions
8. Practice, practice, practice
9. Get a good night's sleep; don't try to cram the night before the test
10. Eat a well balanced meal
11. Know the exact physical location of the testing site; drive the route to the site prior to test day
12. Bring a set of ear plugs; the testing center could be noisy
13. Wear comfortable, loose fitting, layered clothing to the testing center; prepare for it to be either cold or hot during the test
14. Bring at least 2 current forms of ID to the testing center
15. Arrive to the test early; be prepared to wait and be patient
16. Eliminate the obviously wrong answer choices, then guess the first remaining choice
17. Pace yourself; don't rush, but keep working and move on if you get stuck
18. Maintain a positive attitude even if the test is going poorly
19. Keep your first answer unless you are positive it is wrong
20. Check your work, don't make a careless mistake

Special Report: What Your Test Score Will Tell You About Your IQ

Did you know that most standardized tests correlate very strongly with IQ? In fact, your general intelligence is a better predictor of your success than any other factor, and most tests intentionally measure this trait to some degree to ensure that those selected by the test are truly qualified for the test's purposes.

Before we can delve into the relation between your test score and IQ, I will first have to explain what exactly is IQ. Here's the formula:

Your IQ = 100 + (Number of standard deviations below or above the average)*15

Now, let's define standard deviations by using an example. If we have 5 people with 5 different heights, then first we calculate the average. Let's say the average was 65 inches. The standard deviation is the "average distance" away from the average of each of the members. It is a direct measure of variability - if the 5 people included Jackie Chan and Shaquille O'Neal, obviously there's a lot more variability in that group than a group of 5 sisters who are all within 6 inches in height of each other. The standard deviation uses a number to characterize the average range of difference within a group.

A convenient feature of most groups is that they have a "normal" distribution- makes sense that most things would be normal, right? Without getting into a bunch of statistical mumbo-jumbo, you just need to know that if you know the average of the group and the standard deviation, you can successfully predict someone's percentile rank in the group.

Confused? Let me give you an example. If instead of 5 people's heights, we had 100 people, we could figure out their rank in height JUST by knowing the average, standard deviation, and their height. We wouldn't need to know each person's height and manually rank them, we could just predict their rank based on three numbers.

What this means is that you can take your PERCENTILE rank that is often given with your test and relate this to your RELATIVE IQ of people taking the test - that is, your IQ relative to the people taking the test. Obviously, there's no way to know your actual IQ because the people taking a standardized test are usually not very good samples of the general population- many of those with extremely low IQ's never achieve a level of success or competency necessary to complete a typical standardized test. In fact, professional psychologists who measure IQ actually have to use non-written tests that can fairly measure the IQ of those not able to complete a traditional test.

The bottom line is to not take your test score too seriously, but it is fun to compute your "relative IQ" among the people who took the test with you. I've done the calculations below. Just look up your percentile rank in the left and then you'll see your "relative IQ" for your test in the right hand column-

Percentile Rank	Your Relative IQ		Percentile Rank	Your Relative IQ
99	135		59	103
98	131		58	103
97	128		57	103
96	126		56	102
95	125		55	102
94	123		54	102
93	122		53	101
92	121		52	101
91	120		51	100
90	119		50	100
89	118		49	100
88	118		48	99
87	117		47	99
86	116		46	98
85	116		45	98
84	115		44	98
83	114		43	97
82	114		42	97
81	113		41	97
80	113		40	96
79	112		39	96
78	112		38	95
77	111		37	95
76	111		36	95
75	110		35	94
74	110		34	94
73	109		33	93
72	109		32	93
71	108		31	93
70	108		30	92
69	107		29	92
68	107		28	91
67	107		27	91
66	106		26	90
65	106		25	90
64	105		24	89
63	105		23	89
62	105		22	88
61	104		21	88
60	104		20	87

Special Report: What is Test Anxiety and How to Overcome It?

The very nature of tests caters to some level of anxiety, nervousness or tension, just as we feel for any important event that occurs in our lives. A little bit of anxiety or nervousness can be a good thing. It helps us with motivation, and makes achievement just that much sweeter. However, too much anxiety can be a problem; especially if it hinders our ability to function and perform.

"Test anxiety," is the term that refers to the emotional reactions that some test-takers experience when faced with a test or exam. Having a fear of testing and exams is based upon a rational fear, since the test-taker's performance can shape the course of an academic career. Nevertheless, experiencing excessive fear of examinations will only interfere with the test-takers ability to perform, and his/her chances to be successful.

There are a large variety of causes that can contribute to the development and sensation of test anxiety. These include, but are not limited to lack of performance and worrying about issues surrounding the test.

Lack of Preparation

Lack of preparation can be identified by the following behaviors or situations:

Not scheduling enough time to study, and therefore cramming the night before the test or exam
Managing time poorly, to create the sensation that there is not enough time to do everything
Failing to organize the text information in advance, so that the study material consists of the entire text and not simply the pertinent information
Poor overall studying habits

Worrying, on the other hand, can be related to both the test taker, or many other factors around him/her that will be affected by the results of the test. These include worrying about:

Previous performances on similar exams, or exams in general
How friends and other students are achieving
The negative consequences that will result from a poor grade or failure

There are three primary elements to test anxiety. Physical components, which involve the same typical bodily reactions as those to acute anxiety (to be discussed below). Emotional factors have to do with fear or panic. Mental or cognitive issues concerning attention spans and memory abilities.

Physical Signals

There are many different symptoms of test anxiety, and these are not limited to mental and emotional strain. Frequently there are a range of physical signals that will let a test taker know that he/she is suffering from test anxiety. These bodily changes can include the following:

Perspiring
Sweaty palms
Wet, trembling hands
Nausea
Dry mouth
A knot in the stomach
Headache
Faintness
Muscle tension
Aching shoulders, back and neck
Rapid heart beat
Feeling too hot/cold

To recognize the sensation of test anxiety, a test-taker should monitor him/herself for the following sensations:

The physical distress symptoms as listed above
Emotional sensitivity, expressing emotional feelings such as the need to cry or laugh too much, or a sensation of anger or helplessness
A decreased ability to think, causing the test-taker to blank out or have racing thoughts that are hard to organize or control.

Though most students will feel some level of anxiety when faced with a test or exam, the majority can cope with that anxiety and maintain it at a manageable level. However, those who cannot are faced with a very real and very serious condition, which can and should be controlled for the immeasurable benefit of this sufferer.

Naturally, these sensations lead to negative results for the testing experience. The most common effects of test anxiety have to do with nervousness and mental blocking.

Nervousness

Nervousness can appear in several different levels:

The test-taker's difficulty, or even inability to read and understand the questions on the test
The difficulty or inability to organize thoughts to a coherent form
The difficulty or inability to recall key words and concepts relating to the testing questions (especially essays)
The receipt of poor grades on a test, though the test material was well known by the test taker

Conversely, a person may also experience mental blocking, which involves:

Blanking out on test questions
Only remembering the correct answers to the questions when the test has already finished.

Fortunately for test anxiety sufferers, beating these feelings, to a large degree, has to do with proper preparation. When a test taker has a feeling of preparedness, then anxiety will be dramatically lessened.

The first step to resolving anxiety issues is to distinguish which of the two types of anxiety are being suffered. If the anxiety is a direct result of a lack of preparation, this should be considered a normal reaction, and the anxiety level (as opposed to the test results) shouldn't be anything to worry about. However, if, when adequately prepared, the test-taker still panics, blanks out, or seems to overreact, this is not a fully rational reaction. While this can be considered normal too, there are many ways to combat and overcome these effects.

Remember that anxiety cannot be entirely eliminated, however, there are ways to minimize it, to make the anxiety easier to manage. Preparation is one of the best ways to minimize test anxiety. Therefore the following techniques are wise in order to best fight off any anxiety that may want to build.

To begin with, try to avoid cramming before a test, whenever it is possible. By trying to memorize an entire term's worth of information in one day, you'll be shocking your system, and not giving yourself a very good chance to absorb the information. This is an easy path to anxiety, so for those who suffer from test anxiety, cramming should not even be considered an option.

Instead of cramming, work throughout the semester to combine all of the material which is presented throughout the semester, and work on it gradually as the course goes by, making sure to master the main concepts first, leaving minor details for a week or so before the test.

To study for the upcoming exam, be sure to pose questions that may be on the examination, to gauge the ability to answer them by integrating the ideas from your texts, notes and lectures, as well as any supplementary readings.

If it is truly impossible to cover all of the information that was covered in that particular term, concentrate on the most important portions, that can be covered very well. Learn these concepts as best as possible, so that when the test comes, a goal can be made to use these concepts as presentations of your knowledge.

In addition to study habits, changes in attitude are critical to beating a struggle with test anxiety. In fact, an improvement of the perspective over the entire test-taking experience can actually help a test taker to enjoy studying and therefore improve the overall experience. Be certain not to overemphasize the significance of the grade - know that the result of the test is neither a reflection of self worth, nor is it a measure of intelligence; one grade will not predict a person's future success.

To improve an overall testing outlook, the following steps should be tried:

Keeping in mind that the most reasonable expectation for taking a test is to expect to try to demonstrate as much of what you know as you possibly can.
Reminding ourselves that a test is only one test; this is not the only one, and there will be others.
The thought of thinking of oneself in an irrational, all-or-nothing term should be avoided at all costs.
A reward should be designated for after the test, so there's something to look forward to. Whether it be going to a movie, going out to eat, or simply visiting friends, schedule it in advance, and do it no matter what result is expected on the exam.

Test-takers should also keep in mind that the basics are some of the most important things, even beyond anti-anxiety techniques and studying. Never neglect the basic social, emotional and biological needs, in order to try to absorb information. In order to best achieve, these three factors must be held as just as important as the studying itself.

Study Steps

Remember the following important steps for studying:

Maintain healthy nutrition and exercise habits. Continue both your recreational activities and social pass times. These both contribute to your physical and emotional well being.
Be certain to get a good amount of sleep, especially the night before the test, because when you're overtired you are not able to perform to the best of your best ability.
Keep the studying pace to a moderate level by taking breaks when they are needed, and varying the work whenever possible, to keep the mind fresh instead of getting bored. When enough studying has been done that all the material that can be learned has been learned, and the test taker is prepared for the test, stop studying and do something relaxing such as listening to music, watching a movie, or taking a warm bubble bath.

There are also many other techniques to minimize the uneasiness or apprehension that is experienced along with test anxiety before, during, or even after the examination. In fact, there are a great deal of things that can be done to stop anxiety from interfering with lifestyle and performance. Again, remember that anxiety will not be eliminated entirely, and it shouldn't be. Otherwise that "up" feeling for exams would not exist, and most of us depend on that sensation to perform better than usual. However, this anxiety has to be at a level that is manageable.

Of course, as we have just discussed, being prepared for the exam is half the battle right away. Attending all classes, finding out what knowledge will be expected on the exam, and knowing the exam schedules are easy steps to lowering anxiety. Keeping up with work will remove the need to cram, and efficient study habits will eliminate wasted time. Studying should be done in an ideal location for concentration, so that it is simple to become interested in the material and give it complete attention. A method such as SQ3R (Survey, Question, Read, Recite, Review) is a wonderful key to follow to make sure that the study habits are as effective as possible, especially in the case of learning from a textbook. Flashcards are great techniques for memorization. Learning to take good notes will mean that notes will be full of useful information, so that less sifting will need to be done to seek out what is pertinent for studying. Reviewing notes after class and then again on occasion will keep the information fresh in the mind. From notes that have been taken summary sheets and outlines can be made for simpler reviewing.

A study group can also be a very motivational and helpful place to study, as there will be a sharing of ideas, all of the minds can work together, to make sure that everyone understands, and the studying will be made more interesting because it will be a social occasion.

Basically, though, as long as the test-taker remains organized and self confident, with efficient study habits, less time will need to be spent studying, and higher grades will be achieved.

To become self confident, there are many useful steps. The first of these is "self talk." It has been shown through extensive research, that self-talk for students who suffer from test anxiety, should be well monitored, in order to make sure that it contributes to self confidence as opposed to sinking the student. Frequently the self talk of test-anxious students is negative or self-defeating, thinking that everyone else is smarter and faster, that they always mess up, and that if they don't do well, they'll fail the entire course. It is important to decreasing anxiety that awareness is made of self talk. Try writing any negative self thoughts and then disputing them with a positive statement instead. Begin self-encouragement as though it was a friend speaking. Repeat positive statements to help reprogram the mind to believing in successes instead of failures.

Helpful Techniques

Other extremely helpful techniques include:

Self-visualization of doing well and reaching goals
While aiming for an "A" level of understanding, don't try to "overprotect" by setting your expectations lower. This will only convince the mind to stop studying in order to meet the lower expectations.
Don't make comparisons with the results or habits of other students. These are individual factors, and different things work for different people, causing different results.
Strive to become an expert in learning what works well, and what can be done in order to improve. Consider collecting this data in a journal.
Create rewards for after studying instead of doing things before studying that will only turn into avoidance behaviors.
Make a practice of relaxing - by using methods such as progressive relaxation, self-hypnosis, guided imagery, etc - in order to make relaxation an automatic sensation.
Work on creating a state of relaxed concentration so that concentrating will take on the focus of the mind, so that none will be wasted on worrying.
Take good care of the physical self by eating well and getting enough sleep.
Plan in time for exercise and stick to this plan.

Beyond these techniques, there are other methods to be used before, during and after the test that will help the test-taker perform well in addition to overcoming anxiety. Before the exam comes the academic preparation. This involves establishing a study schedule and beginning at least one week before the actual date of the test. By doing this, the anxiety of not having enough time to study for the test will be automatically eliminated. Moreover, this will make the studying a much more effective experience, ensuring that the learning will be an easier process. This relieves much undue pressure on the test-taker.

Summary sheets, note cards, and flash cards with the main concepts and examples of these main concepts should be prepared in advance of the actual studying time. A topic should never be eliminated from this process. By omitting a topic because it isn't expected to be on the test is only setting up the test-taker for anxiety should it actually appear on the exam. Utilize the course syllabus for laying out the topics that should be studied. Carefully go over the notes that were made in class, paying special attention to any of the issues that the professor took special care to emphasize while lecturing in class. In the textbooks, use the chapter review, or if possible, the chapter tests, to begin your review.

It may even be possible to ask the instructor what information will be covered on the exam, or what the format of the exam will be (for example, multiple choice, essay, free form, true-false). Additionally, see if it is possible to find out how many questions will be on the test. If a review sheet or sample test has been offered by the professor, make good use of it, above anything else, for the preparation for the test. Another great resource for getting to know the examination is reviewing tests from previous semesters. Use these tests to review, and aim to achieve a 100% score on each of the possible topics. With a few exceptions, the goal that you set for yourself is the highest one that you will reach.

Take all of the questions that were assigned as homework, and rework them to any other possible course material. The more problems reworked, the more skill and confidence will form as a result. When forming the solution to a problem, write out each of the steps. Don't simply do head work. By doing as many steps on paper as possible, much clarification and therefore confidence will be formed. Do this with as many homework problems as possible, before checking the answers. By checking the answer after each problem, a reinforcement will exist, that will not be on the exam. Study situations should be as exam-like as possible, to prime the test-taker's system for the experience. By waiting to check the answers at the end, a psychological advantage will be formed, to decrease the stress factor.

Another fantastic reason for not cramming is the avoidance of confusion in concepts, especially when it comes to mathematics. 8-10 hours of study will become one hundred percent more effective if it is spread out over a week or at least several days, instead of doing it all in one sitting. Recognize that the human brain requires time in order to assimilate new material, so frequent breaks and a span of study time over several days will be much more beneficial.

Additionally, don't study right up until the point of the exam. Studying should stop a minimum of one hour before the exam begins. This allows the brain to rest and put things in their proper order. This will also provide the time to become as relaxed as

- 80 -

possible when going into the examination room. The test-taker will also have time to eat well and eat sensibly. Know that the brain needs food as much as the rest of the body. With enough food and enough sleep, as well as a relaxed attitude, the body and the mind are primed for success.

Avoid any anxious classmates who are talking about the exam. These students only spread anxiety, and are not worth sharing the anxious sentimentalities.

Before the test also involves creating a positive attitude, so mental preparation should also be a point of concentration. There are many keys to creating a positive attitude. Should fears become rushing in, make a visualization of taking the exam, doing well, and seeing an A written on the paper. Write out a list of affirmations that will bring a feeling of confidence, such as "I am doing well in my English class," "I studied well and know my material," "I enjoy this class." Even if the affirmations aren't believed at first, it sends a positive message to the subconscious which will result in an alteration of the overall belief system, which is the system that creates reality.

If a sensation of panic begins, work with the fear and imagine the very worst! Work through the entire scenario of not passing the test, failing the entire course, and dropping out of school, followed by not getting a job, and pushing a shopping cart through the dark alley where you'll live. This will place things into perspective! Then, practice deep breathing and create a visualization of the opposite situation - achieving an "A" on the exam, passing the entire course, receiving the degree at a graduation ceremony.

On the day of the test, there are many things to be done to ensure the best results, as well as the most calm outlook. The following stages are suggested in order to maximize test-taking potential:

Begin the examination day with a moderate breakfast, and avoid any coffee or beverages with caffeine if the test taker is prone to jitters. Even people who are used to managing caffeine can feel jittery or light-headed when it is taken on a test day.
Attempt to do something that is relaxing before the examination begins. As last minute cramming clouds the mastering of overall concepts, it is better to use this time to create a calming outlook.
Be certain to arrive at the test location well in advance, in order to provide time to select a location that is away from doors, windows and other distractions, as well as giving enough time to relax before the test begins.
Keep away from anxiety generating classmates who will upset the sensation of stability and relaxation that is being attempted before the exam.
Should the waiting period before the exam begins cause anxiety, create a self-distraction by reading a light magazine or something else that is relaxing and simple.

During the exam itself, read the entire exam from beginning to end, and find out how much time should be allotted to each individual problem. Once writing the exam, should more time be taken for a problem, it should be abandoned, in order to begin another problem. If there is time at the end, the unfinished problem can always be returned to and completed.

Read the instructions very carefully - twice - so that unpleasant surprises won't follow during or after the exam has ended.

When writing the exam, pretend that the situation is actually simply the completion of homework within a library, or at home. This will assist in forming a relaxed atmosphere, and will allow the brain extra focus for the complex thinking function.

Begin the exam with all of the questions with which the most confidence is felt. This will build the confidence level regarding the entire exam and will begin a quality momentum. This will also create encouragement for trying the problems where uncertainty resides.

Going with the "gut instinct" is always the way to go when solving a problem. Second guessing should be avoided at all costs. Have confidence in the ability to do well.

For essay questions, create an outline in advance that will keep the mind organized and make certain that all of the points are remembered. For multiple choice, read every answer, even if the correct one has been spotted - a better one may exist.

Continue at a pace that is reasonable and not rushed, in order to be able to work carefully. Provide enough time to go over the answers at the end, to check for small errors that can be corrected.

Should a feeling of panic begin, breathe deeply, and think of the feeling of the body releasing sand through its pores. Visualize a calm, peaceful place, and include all of the sights, sounds and sensations of this image. Continue the deep breathing, and take a few minutes to continue this with closed eyes. When all is well again, return to the test.

If a "blanking" occurs for a certain question, skip it and move on to the next question. There will be time to return to the other question later. Get everything done that can be done, first, to guarantee all the grades that can be compiled, and to build all of the confidence possible. Then return to the weaker questions to build the marks from there.

Remember, one's own reality can be created, so as long as the belief is there, success will follow. And remember: anxiety can happen later, right now, there's an exam to be written!

After the examination is complete, whether there is a feeling for a good grade or a bad grade, don't dwell on the exam, and be certain to follow through on the reward that was promised...and enjoy it! Don't dwell on any mistakes that have been made, as there is nothing that can be done at this point anyway.

Additionally, don't begin to study for the next test right away. Do something relaxing for a while, and let the mind relax and prepare itself to begin absorbing information again.

From the results of the exam - both the grade and the entire experience, be certain to learn from what has gone on. Perfect studying habits and work some more on confidence in order to make the next examination experience even better than the last one.

Learn to avoid places where openings occurred for laziness, procrastination and day dreaming.

Use the time between this exam and the next one to better learn to relax, even learning to relax on cue, so that any anxiety can be controlled during the next exam. Learn how to relax the body. Slouch in your chair if that helps. Tighten and then relax all of the different muscle groups, one group at a time, beginning with the feet and then working all the way up to the neck and face. This will ultimately relax the muscles more than they were to begin with. Learn how to breathe deeply and comfortably, and focus on this breathing going in and out as a relaxing thought. With every exhale, repeat the word "relax."

As common as test anxiety is, it is very possible to overcome it. Make yourself one of the test-takers who overcome this frustrating hindrance.

Special Report: Retaking the Test: What Are Your Chances at Improving Your Score?

After going through the experience of taking a major test, many test takers feel that once is enough. The test usually comes during a period of transition in the test taker's life, and taking the test is only one of a series of important events. With so many distractions and conflicting recommendations, it may be difficult for a test taker to rationally determine whether or not he should retake the test after viewing his scores.

The importance of the test usually only adds to the burden of the retake decision. However, don't be swayed by emotion. There a few simple questions that you can ask yourself to guide you as you try to determine whether a retake would improve your score:

1. What went wrong? Why wasn't your score what you expected?

Can you point to a single factor or problem that you feel caused the low score? Were you sick on test day? Was there an emotional upheaval in your life that caused a distraction? Were you late for the test or not able to use the full time allotment? If you can point to any of these specific, individual problems, then a retake should definitely be considered.

2. Is there enough time to improve?

Many problems that may show up in your score report may take a lot of time for improvement. A deficiency in a particular math skill may require weeks or months of tutoring and studying to improve. If you have enough time to improve an identified weakness, then a retake should definitely be considered.

3. How will additional scores be used? Will a score average, highest score, or most recent score be used?

Different test scores may be handled completely differently. If you've taken the test multiple times, sometimes your highest score is used, sometimes your average score is computed and used, and sometimes your most recent score is used. Make sure you understand what method will be used to evaluate your scores, and use that to help you determine whether a retake should be considered.

4. Are my practice test scores significantly higher than my actual test score?

If you have taken a lot of practice tests and are consistently scoring at a much higher level than your actual test score, then you should consider a retake. However, if you've taken five practice tests and only one of your scores was higher than your actual test score, or if your practice test scores were only slightly higher than your actual test score, then it is unlikely that you will significantly increase your score.

5. Do I need perfect scores or will I be able to live with this score? Will this score still allow me to follow my dreams?

What kind of score is acceptable to you? Is your current score "good enough?" Do you have to have a certain score in order to pursue the future of your dreams? If you won't be happy with your current score, and there's no way that you could live with it, then you should consider a retake. However, don't get your hopes up. If you are looking for significant improvement, that may or may not be possible. But if you won't be happy otherwise, it is at least worth the effort.
Remember that there are other considerations. To achieve your dream, it is likely that your grades may also be taken into account. A great test score is usually not the only thing necessary to succeed. Make sure that you aren't overemphasizing the importance of a high test score.

Furthermore, a retake does not always result in a higher score. Some test takers will score lower on a retake, rather than higher. One study shows that one-fourth of test takers will achieve a significant improvement in test score, while one-sixth of test takers will actually show a decrease. While this shows that most test takers will improve, the majority will only improve their scores a little and a retake may not be worth the test taker's effort.

Finally, if a test is taken only once and is considered in the added context of good grades on the part of a test taker, the person reviewing the grades and scores may be tempted to assume that the test taker just had a bad day while taking the test, and may discount the low test score in favor of the high grades. But if the test is retaken and the scores are approximately the same, then the validity of the low scores are only confirmed. Therefore, a retake could actually hurt a test taker by definitely bracketing a test taker's score ability to a limited range.

Special Report: Additional Bonus Material

Due to our efforts to try to keep this book to a manageable length, we've created a link that will give you access to all of your additional bonus material.

Please visit http://www.mometrix.com/bonus948/vsolg4math to access the information.